MW00790674

Dwight F. Burlingame, Timothy L. Seiler,
Eugene R. Tempel
Indiana University Center on Philanthropy
EDITORS

CAPITAL CAMPAIGNS

REALIZING THEIR POWER AND POTENTIAL

Andrea Kihlstedt
Consultant

Robert Pierpont
Pierpont & Wilkerson, Ltd.

EDITORS

NUMBER 21, FALL 1998

CAPITAL CAMPAIGNS: REALIZING THEIR POWER AND POTENTIAL
Andrea Kihlstedt, Robert Pierpont (eds.)
New Directions for Philanthropic Fundraising, No. 21, Fall 1998
Dwight F. Burlingame, Timothy L. Seiler, Eugene R. Tempel, Editors

NEW DIRECTIONS FOR PHILANTHROPIC FUNDRAISING is indexed in Higher Education
Abstracts and Philanthropic Index.

Microfilm copies of issues and articles are available in 16 mm and 35 mm, as well as
microfiche in 105 mm, through University Microfilms Inc., 300 North Zeeb Road,
Ann Arbor, Michigan 48106-1346.

ISSN 1072-172X   ISBN 0-7879-4269-3

NEW DIRECTIONS FOR PHILANTHROPIC FUNDRAISING is part of The Jossey-Bass
Nonprofit Sector Series and is published quarterly by Jossey-Bass Inc., Publishers,
350 Sansome Street, San Francisco, California 94104-1342.

SUBSCRIPTIONS cost $67.00 for individuals and $115.00 for institutions, agencies,
and libraries. Prices subject to change. Refer to the Ordering Information page
at the back of this issue.

EDITORIAL CORRESPONDENCE should be sent to the editor, Dwight F. Burlingame,
Center on Philanthropy, Indiana University, 550 West North Street, Suite 301,
Indianapolis, IN 46202-3162.

www.josseybass.com

Printed in the United States of America on acid-free recycled paper containing 100
percent recovered waste paper, of which at least 20 percent is postconsumer waste.

Contents

Editors' Notes

IN PLANNING the capital campaign issue of this journal, we have had an opportunity to stand back from the field in which both of us are engaged day to day as consultants and teachers. We took ourselves "out of the fray" for a bit and explored the many aspects of capital campaign fundraising that we might address. Our list was lengthy, ranging from the philosophical to the practical, from the transformational to the mundane. After much discussion, we decided to solicit chapters that dealt with three subjects: the transformational power of campaigns, technical aspects of campaign fundraising, and the application of campaign techniques to nontraditional organizations. We then invited experts—development professionals, consultants, foundation directors, and college presidents—to write chapters in which they would share their extensive knowledge and experience.

We have been rewarded with an excellent collection that both reinforces principles of capital campaign fundraising and provides new insights into the field. The first two chapters address the transformational nature of campaign fundraising. In Chapter One, "Thinking Beyond the Dollar Goal: A Campaign as Organizational Transformation," Carol O'Brien explores the power of a campaign to push an organization to reexplore its mission and vision. In Chapter Two, "Dynamics of the Challenge Grant," John Marshall and Eugene Tempel discuss the transformational value of the challenge grant strategy when applied to campaigns. Using The Kresge Foundation model as their example, they show how challenge grants can help organizations do far more than raise money.

The next three chapters focus on specific aspects of capital campaign fundraising: leadership gifts, goal setting, and information

NEW DIRECTIONS FOR PHILANTHROPIC FUNDRAISING, NO. 21, FALL 1998 © JOSSEY-BASS PUBLISHERS

management. Rodney Kirsch and Martin Shell wrote Chapter Three, "Achieving Leadership Gifts: The Investment Returns of Lasting Relationships," a powerful reminder that leadership gifts are investments that have both value for the donor and meaning for the organization. In Chapter Four, Robert Pierpont and Steven Wilkerson focus on the complexities of setting and resetting campaign goals as "Campaign Goals: Taking Aim at a Moving Target" explores the critical processes of goal setting and testing. In Chapter Five, "Information Systems: Managing the Database," Scott Lange and Charles Hunsaker take us from the sublime of leadership gifts to perhaps a more mundane but essential aspect of campaign fundraising as they explore the use of computer systems to manage the myriad pieces of information generated during a campaign and discuss the complex issues that arise when preparing the information management system for the increased load of a campaign.

The final chapter, Chapter Six, "Working from Strength: How Small Organizations Succeed with Big Campaigns," by Christine Graham, recognizes that many small and inexperienced organizations are trying their hands at capital campaign fundraising. Graham provides an excellent discussion of the campaign process when it is applied to these small grassroots or neophyte organizations.

The Introduction to this volume was written by John Synodinos, who has eloquently and succinctly created a context for the chapters that follow. He has unfolded for us the history of capital campaign fundraising, spelled out the characteristics common to all campaigns, and summarized the rather astonishing power of this form of fundraising.

We extend our heartfelt thanks to all of the authors who contributed to this volume. Through their writing, we have come to understand and appreciate our field better!

Andrea Kihlstedt
Robert Pierpont
Editors

ANDREA KIHLSTEDT *writes, teaches, and consults on capital campaign fundraising. She lives and works in Lancaster, Pennsylvania, and New York City.*

ROBERT PIERPONT *is chairman and CEO of Pierpont & Wilkerson, Ltd., a fundraising consulting firm based outside of New York City in Garrison, New York.*

Introduction

John Synodinos

THOUGH THE PRACTICE OF FUNDRAISING is older than the millennium, the capital campaign is a relatively recent invention. In the late nineteenth century, two YMCA directors, Lyman Pierce of Omaha, Nebraska, and Charles S. Ward of Grand Rapids, Michigan, tired of spending nearly all their time and efforts on building membership and independently developed a process that contained the essential elements of what has come to be known as the capital campaign. Their process included setting goals to be achieved, organizing volunteers trained and willing to make calls, carefully drawing a timetable with specific deadlines, preparing a case statement written from the point of view of the prospect, holding screening meetings and kickoff events, assigning prospects, holding report meetings, and having a final victory celebration.

At the turn of the century, the New York City YMCA used the process to raise the funds needed for constructing a new building. The process was first adapted to higher education when the University of Pittsburgh borrowed one of the two directors to raise the monies needed to build that institution's "cathedral of learning."

The capital campaign has had an enormous impact on the direction of American society in the twentieth century. Indeed, it is difficult to imagine the private sector of higher education, for example, having survived without the funds that came as a consequence of capital campaigns—funds for campus buildings, equipment, and endowment. However, this "invention" not only benefitted colleges and universities but was and continues to be

NEW DIRECTIONS FOR PHILANTHROPIC FUNDRAISING, NO. 21, FALL 1998 © JOSSEY-BASS PUBLISHERS

employed successfully by virtually every type of educational, religious, and health and human service organization in America.

Although its YMCA inventors would still recognize their progeny, the capital campaign has evolved steadily over the years, easily adapting to meet new categories of organizations and ever-changing societal conditions. Today's campaigns are longer, have higher goals, involve more professional staff, make extensive use of technology, rely more on prospect research, and place more emphasis on the larger gifts. In addition to cash and pledges, campaign totals now include a sizable percentage of planned gifts, real estate and other gifts-in-kind, and even bequests.

The needs to be met have also changed. No longer are campaigns solely about bricks and mortar. Endowments, venture capital funds, equipment, and infrastructure costs are all likely objectives to be reached through a capital campaign. Today's capital campaign is a potent instrument employed by thousands of organizations raising billions of dollars.

A well-executed campaign has many advantages. Campaigns focus attention on an organization, unite its constituencies in a common cause, and raise the sights of donors. Successful campaigns strengthen staff morale, identify new leadership, and result in new annual fund prospects. Beyond a doubt, capital campaigns are the most cost-efficient means of raising funds that exists.

But these many accomplishments, even when taken together, pale beside the significant impact a capital campaign can have on an organization. It is in the planning and rethinking necessitated in the very early stages of a campaign that it can provide the means actually to transform an organization.

Now, as we near the conclusion of the twentieth century, capital campaign fundraising has matured into a primary development tool. More and more, development professionals adapt the powerful lessons of capital campaigns to every aspect of their fundraising programs. We have learned the power of planning and discipline. We have come to understand the mutual opportunities that come from building real and lasting relationships with our donors. And we have learned to see campaign-style fundraising as not just a way to raise money but also as a means of shaping and directing our institutions so that they continue to meet the real needs of our world.

JOHN SYNODINOS *is President Emeritus of Lebanon Valley College, Annville, Pennsylvania, and a principal of the Franklin Consulting Group.*

Campaigns are not primarily about raising money. They are catalysts for organizational change and transformation, providing opportunities for sustained focus on vision and values.

1

Thinking beyond the dollar goal: A campaign as organizational transformation

Carol L. O'Brien

PERIODICALLY, DEVELOPMENT PROFESSIONALS have debated whether campaigns are still viable, whether they remain the best models for raising significant private support, or whether other formats or approaches may be more effective. Perhaps many of these professionals were simply weary of the omnipresent campaign, even though for development officers successful campaign experience became the coin of the realm.

Volunteers and presidents have been more divided in their views. Those who served on campaigns were pleased when they were over; novices were eager to prove themselves. Depending on the critical mass of each faction and the financial needs of the organization, institutional leaders might avoid campaign planning or march ill-prepared into announcement of the public phase.

One thing is now clear. We have moved into an era where the equation reads *campaigns = money.* The major donor and the

NEW DIRECTIONS FOR PHILANTHROPIC FUNDRAISING, NO. 21, FALL 1998 © JOSSEY-BASS PUBLISHERS

public at large have come to understand the campaign model. They can be relied on to react to its signals and phases—from the nucleus fund period for leadership givers and insiders to the public phase and finale for the broad base of annual fund donors and members.

But in taking a longer and more dispassionate view of the campaign phenomenon, we can also see that the ability of this model to raise funds, although effective, pales in comparison with its ability to be a catalyst for organizational change. By forcing an organization to develop a sustained focus on vision and values, major campaigns can transform institutions.

Campaigns and transformation

To gear up for a successful campaign, most organizations now realize they must undertake effective strategic planning. To put it candidly, if all organizations periodically could find the desire or resolve to conduct such planning without the impetus of a campaign, we might witness fewer campaigns. Often the campaign first drives the plan and then drives all of the institutional activity and resources allocated to it. Although the campaign is viewed as the end, it is actually the means. In mobilizing for a campaign, organizations often create the structure and culture they require to help them move into a new stage of development. Campaigns force organizations to differentiate themselves from their competition, establish benchmarks and rites of passage, and organize celebrations and events that codify their progress.

Campaigns compel organizations to carry out processes that a truly effective organization can and should do in the ordinary course of carrying out its business. Many organizations, however, require a campaign to stimulate these activities. For with a campaign in the offing, the financial stakes and rewards are high enough to command the attention of the leadership and the commitment of institutional resources. A campaign pushes an organization to do the following:

- Clarify and affirm the organization's identity
- Generate a strategic plan and vision
- Develop a long-range fiscal plan, showing economic models and trade-offs
- Differentiate and position the organization in the marketplace
- Enlist and engage voluntary and organizational leadership
- Provide support and counsel for the organization's leadership
- Commit financial and staff resources
- Evaluate and adapt the development and communications functions

In sum, the decision to undertake a campaign generates a new level of dialogue and consensus for the organization, both internally and externally. Even in the most decentralized and disparate institutions, campaigns require a sustained focus, an element that may be absent in a noncampaign setting. Thus, the campaign has a galvanizing impact and value well beyond the resources it will engender.

Organizational response to change

In an environment of unrelenting change, financial pressures, and intense public scrutiny, it is understandable that organizations often respond ineffectively to the need for solid planning and change. Some appear defensive or arrogant. Some have lapses in judgment or integrity in the performance of their fiduciary or constituency responsibilities. Many have escaped into silence, turning inward—losing their organizational voice.

This is not to imply that charitable organizations are not frantically busy and enormously productive; what it does imply is that the context for and the communication of our outcomes have become blurred. This lack of focus is often debilitating. Staff members lose sight of primary objectives, volunteers become dispirited, and leaders become ineffective. And with blurred outcomes, organizations lose the ability to celebrate real accomplishments.

When a campaign helps an organization clarify and recommit to its values and define specific outcomes, it also enables that organization to reclaim its sense of direction and worth.

Reclaiming the organizational voice

If the strategic planning process that precedes the campaign process dwells on money and dollar goals, the organization misses an opportunity to define and articulate its more substantive, inspirational goals. The way in which an organization communicates its goal sends a powerful message about its values and becomes a kind of self-fulfilling prophecy. An organization that overemphasizes its monetary objectives often does not draw its constituents into the deeper commitment that comes from sharing in its values and mission. First and foremost, therefore, the campaign helps reclaim an organizational voice that speaks of the best and highest aspirations of an organization, not merely its financial needs or goals.

Starting with the strategic plan

The strategic plan, or long-range plan, is a set of objectives that emanate from an organization's mission but capitalize on the external opportunities and challenges that the organization faces. Even when the motivation for a strategic plan is the desire to begin a campaign, the focus of the plan should not be financial. Development officers and even CEOs must resist the pressure to answer the inevitable question, "How much can we raise?" before fully exploring the more substantive issues that should undergird the planning process. Campaign materials—a gift table, volunteer organization chart, and crediting policies—belong in the campaign planning process, not in the strategic plan.

A strategic plan should be deemed so essential to the future of the organization that the board and administration are willing to fund it from reallocations and other revenue streams, including but not limited to philanthropy. Trustees, foundation directors, presidents of other nonprofits, academic leaders, and consultants are often enlisted in the planning process to ensure that the level of discourse remains substantive, rooted in the institution's mission and relevant to its constituency.

The development professional and the strategic plan

Development professionals play a vital role in the process of redefining and transforming the organization. However, although they are often ideally suited to assume the leadership role in strategic planning, the fundraising staff must not be seen as the sole agent or owner of the plan. Too direct a role by the development staff in the strategic planning process might be misconstrued as self-serving. On the one hand, an overly involved development staff might be viewed as using the process to become more visible. On the other hand, the staff might be suspected of limiting the scope of planning objectives for fear that they will be unable to raise the money needed for ambitious goals.

An organization's academic leadership must define and deliver on the organization's mission. If the leadership is not actively invested in the planning process, regardless of the resources raised the institution will not have a clear sense of the outcomes toward which the new resources should be applied. The institution and the development professional are best served when development is a partner in the strategic planning process but not its creator.

Benefits of an inclusive planning process

Although there are probably as many forms of strategic planning as there are organizations or strategic planners, the most effective processes are inclusive but have a strong top-down orientation. If the exercise is simply a percolation of loosely evaluated needs, there is little chance that a broad and engaging vision will emanate from it. A shopping list approach devalues the process. Done well, an inclusive process results in several outcomes:

- It reaffirms organizational values.
- It creates stakeholders and beneficiaries.
- It acts as a reality check.
- It evaluates the current enterprise and forces decision making.
- It stimulates new approaches and initiatives.
- It coalesces the common vision.
- It creates spokespeople for the plan.
- It fosters the engagement that leads to philanthropy.

Listening to your constituents

Even an inclusive strategic planning process can be too internally focused. The loyal, insider board members may be too close to provide objective scrutiny of performance, opportunities, and choices. Indeed, some may be emotionally invested in the organization in ways that, although productive, also can be self-limiting. Therefore, both the process and the dialogue must be opened up to a broader cross section of constituents. Setting the stage for these conversations in an atmosphere of respect and trust is one of the early positive results of preparing for a campaign.

Selecting the participants and the form for the planning sessions requires a strategic framework and political sensitivity. The organization does not want to preach to the converted or overlook the experienced members in the larger community. If the organization requires assistance in particular areas, the planning process might be used to involve representatives from those sectors. If, for example, an organization is trying to build visibility with the corporate community, the planning process provides opportunities to invite business leaders to engage in the assessment. In selecting the planning group mentors, the organization must balance access with productive engagement. Should the organization seek a blue-ribbon panel of external experts that can enhance its visibility or a less well-known but more knowledgeable and available group of advisers? When recruiting the committee members, the organization has an opportunity to match the participants to its specific needs. It might reach out broadly or it might focus tightly on targeted fields of expertise; either method can be valid within the context of a given organization.

The form of planning conversations is also important. Task forces on subsets of issues may later be integrated into a larger plan and discussion. Surveys and focus groups gather even more external feedback. Ultimately, the planning process results in an exchange of ideas, aspirations, issues, and data. These elements are synthesized into a document with specific objectives (qualitative and quantitative) and a set of financial requirements, both of which are to be achieved over a defined period of time.

Facing difficult issues

Occasionally strategic planning is problematic. On the surface, people may agree that the institution needs to make changes—eliminate some programs or services, clarify its identity, even reorganize its governance structure. But underneath the surface the status quo is difficult to change, and implementing the new directions that come from effective planning can become challenging.

The process of strategic planning followed by a campaign usually forces organizations to deal with difficult issues. In many cases, old problems that people have become somewhat reconciled to or are unwilling to address resurface. These issues may acquire a greater urgency or significance when examined in the context of strategic or long-range planning. The classic example is the composition of an organization's board. In too many settings board members are not recruited or expected to assume a role in advancement. Members may go years without even being asked to make a gift. In the face of a strategic plan and subsequent campaign, giving is no longer optional for board members.

Often consultants are forewarned that interviewees in a feasibility study may have specific concerns about board giving that
are then corroborated during the study meetings. If these concerns were anticipated, why did the organization avoid dealing
with them for so long? Human nature, politics, and resources are
some of the answers. But the most important missing ingredient
is often the lack of a mandate for change. The strategic planning
process dictates change and thus provides the rationale to con-
front difficult problems. The engagement and consensus of a
strong planning committee further mandates dealing with difficult issues. An inclusive planning process reaffirms an organization's strengths and assesses its weaknesses, renewing its abilities
to address both.

Sometimes strategic planning followed by campaign studies clar-
ifies the "real problems." Often an organization's leaders believes
that the institution is at a competitive disadvantage for one reason
when in fact they have a misperception with which to contend. For
example, in one study we conducted for a hospital, the CEO and
development staff briefed us that they believed they were losing
patients because the quality of their facilities had declined. But in
our interviews, former patients told a different story: they were
reluctant to seek care at the hospital because there had been a number of significant retirements among the longtime medical staff.
Patients were more concerned about no longer "knowing their doctors" than about the hospital not having state-of-the-art treatment
facilities.

Although the hospital embarked on and successfully completed a
campaign for facilities, it was based on a public education campaign
and a case for support that emphasized the high-quality care that
would be offered by the recently arrived physicians, who were committed to staying in the community. The personalities and creden-
tials of the physicians were highlighted and the physicians were
encouraged to take on more visible roles in the community, such
as joining civic organizations. The doctors even decided to show
their support for their new community and its hospital by giving
generously to the campaign.

If not a strategic plan, then at least a strategic direction

Despite our best and most persuasive reasoning, sometimes development professionals and consultants cannot convince an organization to undertake strategic planning. When this is the situation, we should at least help shape a statement of strategic direction. It may be that the board and staff revisit the mission statement during a retreat or that a short-term task force counsels the organization on new opportunities for marketing or generating revenue.

No matter how it is orchestrated, the transformational effect of a campaign will not be felt unless some degree of strategic forethought is given to the institution's identity and future. Without this kind of dialogue, resources are often secured for less significant or even the wrong purposes, and the real benefits of these resources may be marginal or misguided.

Leadership: The sine qua non of the transformation

No matter whether an organization develops a full strategic plan or merely a statement of strategic direction, leadership is the essential ingredient. The strategic planning period provides excellent opportunities to recruit and try out new leadership. With a mandate to evaluate and position the organization, the institution should be able to attract individuals whose stature and perspective can both complement and stimulate its current leadership.

The selection of leadership for this process is both art and science. Naturally, strong individuals with backgrounds in business and other fields that relate to the organization's mission are important. Creative and expressive people, regardless of their background, are also vital to the process because they will speak from the heart and spirit as well as from the mind.

The structure of the planning group can take many forms—steering committee, task force, or blue-ribbon panel—but its process is an alchemical one. With thoughtful and dedicated direction, this body can explore the full scope of programmatic, financial, ethical, and competitive issues that an organization is confronting.

Differentiating the organization: The identity statement

The discussions that ensue during the strategic planning process are the key to assessing and concurring on the strategic direction and, ultimately, on the strategic plan. At the heart of these conversations are the perceptions that each member holds of the institution's identity. As the group explores the core values that foster this identity, they can come to agreement on a simple statement that differentiates the organization from its peers. The objective of the identity statement is to communicate the organization's salient characteristics and services. It will take time to draft the statement, and the statement will continue to evolve as it is communicated to different audiences and used for varying purposes. An early version of a statement that is being developed for WGBH, one of the nation's premier public broadcasting stations, is as follows:

WGBH is a content provider for public broadcasting, producing one-third of the nation's prime-time programming seen nationally on PBS and contributing to programming for national public radio. WGBH extends its educational impact beyond the airwaves through outlets that reach millions more via books, CD-ROMs, teacher's guides, and on-line services. WGBH made television accessible by developing captioning for America's deaf or hard-of-hearing citizens and pioneering descriptive video service for the blind and visually impaired.
Produced in Boston, shared with the nation.

The last phrase is a tag line that was used in an annual media campaign in Boston for WGBH. However, the phrase could easily become a campaign theme, demonstrating the important link between the identity statement and the substance of a campaign.

Because organizations are, after all, basically tribes, their stories are vital. If organizations stop telling their stories, they lose their history; some might say they also lose their dreams and their futures.

This is an aspect of the loss of organizational voice described earlier. However, as the planning process draws on the organization's history and core values, it also revitalizes its organizational voice.

For some, the identity and messages come through more vividly in visual images. Photographs can be poignant, drawings and logos can be persuasive, diagrams can simplify the most complicated concepts.

Outcomes of the communications process

The deliberations that the organization undertakes, and the verbal and visual representations that emanate from them, clarify and give new meaning to the organization's activities. These representations are placed in a context and a continuum that a wider audience can understand. In clarifying its message, the organization has the opportunity to manage the meaning or to "frame" the perceptions that its key audiences hold. Complicated or problematic issues can gain acceptance if they are described in more accessible language over a longer period of time.

The objectives and the choices made in the strategic planning process or the creation of the identity statement are based on a vision of the organization's future. If the process has been satisfying and inclusive, many will have embraced a common vision. When encouraged, they can begin to personalize it. As the physicians mentioned earlier began to treat new patients in their community hospital, those patients could envision a health care organization that would meet their needs in the future. And as the viewers of WGBH watch the station's annual media campaign, they are reminded that they can look forward to quality programming in the future.

Framing the goal

As the organization moves from strategic planning into campaign planning, it formulates a set of monetary and nonmonetary goals for the campaign. These goals are then tested in a feasibility study and again later by the commitments of the leadership donors in the nucleus fund phase of the campaign. The articulation of the campaign goals is an important element in the power of a campaign to transform the organization. If the goal is expressed purely as "dollars to be raised," the character of the campaign becomes competitive, almost commercial. The gifts are communicated as "numbers," whereas recognition of the donors or the uses of the gifts appears as footnotes to those numbers.

However, in those settings where the strategic planning and creation of an identity statement have generated a vision for the organization's future, the goal need not be communicated as purely financial. Rather, there is the opportunity for a more substantive and inspirational approach. The goal can draw attention to the positive outcomes that the campaign gifts will help generate. The gifts, like the campaign, are a means to an end, not an end in themselves.

Although many will bemoan the difficulty of arriving at a successful campaign theme or slogan, if the work has been done on the organization's identity statement, a compelling, unique theme can emerge that will capture the spirit of the campaign and the value of the organization. For example, one of our hospital clients conducted an engaging and extraordinarily successful campaign for its pediatrics department; its theme was *Caring for Kids.*

Nonmonetary goals of a campaign

A campaign may include specific programmatic objectives that advance the organization's mission. Compelling nonmonetary goals can help transform an organization in many ways that often prove as important as its monetary goals. For example, a statement of campaign objectives might include some or all of following:

- Enhance the governance structure
- Strengthen the voluntary leadership
- Create better working relationships
- Establish a better balance between centralized and decentralized functions, such as the development operation

- Invest in new information systems
- Become more proficient in information technology
- Build greater public awareness
- Provide professional development opportunities for staff

When the organization determines, communicates, and invests in a set of nonmonetary objectives, they have as palpable an effect as the philanthropic resources secured by the campaign.

Which goals are transformational?

Although we cannot undervalue the tremendous financial resources and stability that result from successful campaigns, in themselves these resources may not have the capacity to change an organization's culture or image. If there has been solid strategic planning, the campaign builds on that vision and positions the institution to tell its story to a more engaged audience. However, if the organization has also achieved a number of nonmonetary goals, such as strengthening its voluntary leadership or clarifying its identity, the nature of the organization and its future is altered in ways more far-reaching than financial success.

In conclusion, campaigns and the strategic planning required to prepare for them can revitalize organizations in more significant ways than the simple campaign = dollars equation expresses. They help an organization find its collective voice; they provide the opportunity to examine and reshape the institution's programs; they provide mechanisms by which organizations can share and communicate their vision, objectives, and outcomes; and they involve constituents in meaningful initiatives and create reasons and occasions for celebration. Campaigns compel an institution to do the vital work it needs to do in evaluating its programs and potential. In sum, campaigns give voice to the institution's vision, direction, and values.

CAROL L. O'BRIEN *is president of Carol O'Brien Associates, a develop-ment consulting firm that serves clients in higher education, health care, the arts, advocacy, public broadcasting, and human services. The firm has offices in Ithaca, New York, and Durham, North Carolina.*

Challenge grants add to the call for action in a capital campaign, but they can have a more significant impact on long-term organizational development than on the immediate capital campaign.

2

Dynamics of the challenge grant

John E. Marshall III, Eugene R. Tempel

CAPITAL CAMPAIGNS have generally been considered among the most sophisticated fundraising activities undertaken by nonprofit organizations. Where the annual operating fund drive seeks funds to carry out current programs, the capital campaign has been the mechanism for nonprofit organizations to develop their long-term facility and equipment needs, including facility renovation and equipment upgrading and replacement (Rosso, 1991, p. 80).

The capital campaign usually requires concentrated dedication of the nonprofit organization's resources for a specific, discrete time period. It draws on the organization's staff, board, and volunteers, and it approaches the organization's most loyal constituents—its donors—for special commitments (The Fund Raising School, 1998, pp. 99–112).

As a fundraising strategy, the capital campaign has several advantages. First, it generally has a concrete and visible goal in the form of facilities or equipment (and sometimes endowment), which will be evident to the donors. Second, it has a definite time frame for

Note: We wish to thank Jason Chandler, graduate assistant at the Indiana University Center on Philanthropy, for his help with this chapter.

achieving that goal, which serves as a structure for calling both volunteer solicitors and donors to action. And third, it offers the opportunity for public communication to stimulate donor interest, for donors to challenge each other, and for the campaign to serve as a rallying point for the community (Dove, 1988, p. 11).

The challenge grant or gift has been a commonly used tactic in both capital campaigns and annual fund drives. We are all familiar with the public radio and television campaigns in which a donor challenges a group of donors to match his or her gift in the next hour. Several states have offered matching grants for public university endowment campaigns. Private university alumni have a history of challenging their former classmates in both annual and capital campaigns. The challenge grant enhances the call for action in a capital campaign. As a solicitation tactic, it offers the donor an opportunity to extend the impact of his or her gift.

In reviewing the history of The Kresge Foundation's challenge grants, this chapter explores the impact that these grants can have on capital campaigns and proposes that, given appropriate guidelines, challenge grants can have an even more significant impact on long-term organizational development than on the immediate capital campaign.

The Kresge Foundation Challenge Program

The Kresge Foundation Challenge Program is an independent private foundation begun in 1924 by Sebastian S. Kresge. Located in Troy, Michigan, it makes grants nationally (The Kresge Foundation, 1993). It is interested in contributing to the tradition of civic involvement and prefers to support organizations that have the capacity to increase civic involvement.

The Kresge Foundation is unique in that it makes grants exclusively for capital purposes and its grants are always challenge grants. The foundation awards challenge grants most often for the construction or renovation of buildings but also for the purchase of major equipment and real estate. Kresge challenge grants are intended to stimulate new private gifts during an organized fundraising effort. They offer special opportunities for organizations to build capacity, both by providing funding for enhanced facilities in which to present programs and by strengthening the organization's ability to generate private support. In addition, the Kresge challenge grant program goes beyond the conventional wisdom of capital campaigns to help nonprofit organizations think differently about what the capital campaign can achieve for them.

We believe that capital campaigns are about more than just raising money, more than just the new facility or equipment that will result. If those were the primary goals of the capital campaign we should encourage every organization to seek the largest gifts possible from the fewest number of prospects. This approach would probably deliver at least the minimum amount for the project in the briefest time at the lowest cost. But the single donor-dominated capital campaign does not build the broad base of support or develop the broad ownership that the capital campaign has the ability to deliver.

The Kresge Foundation's application process helps organizations understand that capital campaigns are an opportunity for them to accomplish much more than the immediate capital project. First, the application is an occasion for self-assessment, because the foundation considers proposals only from nonprofit organizations that have the following elements in place:

- Evidence of financial stability
- Stable or increasing demand for programs and services
- Effective board, administrative, and program staff
- A track record of quality programs and services

Many capital campaigns fail because organizations have not adequately assessed themselves in these areas (Dove, 1988, p. 24; Rosso, 1991, pp. 93–95). The Kresge challenge grant process thus helps ensure campaign success by challenging organizations to focus on these issues.

Second, the projects proposed to The Kresge Foundation must also meet certain criteria. The scope of the project must be defined so there is assurance that the cost estimates will hold and the fundraising goal is realistic. All the regulatory approvals must be in place so there will be no construction delays that might increase project costs. Finally, all necessary purchase agreements or purchase options for real estate must be signed. These elements can affect the success of a capital campaign by changing the goal and time line of a project, and the challenge to complete them early can help ensure success with the fundraising effort.

If the organization meets all of these criteria, The Kresge Foundation will consider grant proposals in conjunction with the organization's development of a capital campaign. However, it does not accept a proposal until leadership gifts and pledges are committed. At least 20 percent and sometimes as much as 50 percent of the private fundraising goal should be met before an organization files an application. These leadership gifts—from the organization's board, key individual donors, and possibly corporations and foundations—convey strong validation of the organization and the project that the campaign supports. If the first 20 to 50 percent of the campaign is the result of a single gift, then the campaign may be viewed as donor-driven rather than mission-driven. Using unrestricted gifts from other sources to lead the campaign also does not represent a strong case to Kresge. Here again, the grant application process challenges the organization to conduct an effective capital campaign.

Once the leadership gifts are in place, the organization can apply to The Kresge Foundation for a grant. Typically, the Kresge grant will range from 5 to 10 percent of the total campaign goal and will represent at least one-fifth and not more than one-third of the remaining funds to be raised when the grant is announced.

The application process requires the organization to submit its fundraising plan and time frame for the entire campaign. The plan must include a specific fundraising strategy, and goals for fundraising during the five or six months of the Kresge application process. Before a challenge grant is awarded, the organization must demonstrate that it has made progress on this interim fundraising plan. Evidence that it has been able to carry out its plan during the review period strengthens its case when the grant decision is made.

Once a Kresge challenge grant is awarded, the organization must succeed in raising the total challenge amount within the time frame specified by its campaign plan in order for the Kresge funds to be paid.

The process of applying for a Kresge challenge grant, with its deadlines and requirements for interim goals, can help stimulate commitments from reluctant leadership donors. A Kresge grant also helps reach larger numbers of donors for smaller gifts at the end of the campaign (Kihlstedt and Schwartz, 1997, pp. 8–9).

The energy generated by the larger leadership gifts at the beginning of the campaign has often dissipated by the time the campaign reaches the last phases of solicitation. The excitement of big gift announcements is missing, and other challenge gifts or grants and matching grants may already have been completed. The volunteers and staff may be fatigued from the intensive solicitation work. The Kresge challenge during the last part of the campaign provides a boost of energy to bring it to a conclusion. It also provides an incentive to reach the goal on time. Thus, although challenge grants usually help leverage the larger gifts at the beginning of a campaign, the Kresge challenge enables the smaller donors at the end of a campaign to think of extending their smaller gifts and permits resolicitation of early large gifts for the same purpose.

The usual donor development process in a nonprofit organization is based on recurring levels of involvement with and contributions from the organization's donor constituency (The Fund Raising School, 1998, pp. 1–13). A percentage of donors repeats and increases their gifts over time. The capital campaign seeks larger gifts during a finite period of time from this donor base. The organization often asks its committed donors to use accumulated assets instead of current income to make these gifts. And a common side-benefit of the capital campaign is increased levels of annual operating support from a donor base that has raised its philanthropic giving sights during the campaign.

But the Kresge challenge grant program challenges this assumption. Its premise is that a capital campaign can also be an opportunity to expand an organization's donor base instead of relying only on already-identified donors. The application process focuses on expansion of the donor base. The fundraising plan must outline how new individual donors can be brought into the project. The organization is challenged to pay careful attention to converting the psychological investment that first-time donors make in response to the challenge grant into annual funding and other special opportunities with the organization.

Development incentives

Kresge has no illusions that new donors will provide the lead gifts in a campaign. But with the Kresge challenge during the last half to one-third of the campaign, a challenge grant brings in new donors with the opportunity to increase the impact of smaller gifts. A first-time donor to the campaign at $10,000 will become an annual donor who might twenty years later make a $100,000 special gift and in forty years leave a major bequest to the organization. Although we are not suggesting that the traditional donor development process is not valid, we are suggesting that with proper planning, incentives, and awareness, the capital campaign may bring new donors to the organization. To do this, however, an organization must first create awareness of its mission, programs, and services and be held in high regard by the new constituency.

In making its challenge grants, Kresge sees itself as offering four key incentives, incentives that any challenge grant might offer. The first of these is what we might call the *endorsement factor.* The Kresge challenge adds out-of-town money to the project. It gives the project a "seal of approval" that enhances the confidence of the campaign's volunteer solicitors.

Second is the *opportunity factor.* Fifty percent of Kresge grants are to first-time grantees. The challenge grant is an opportunity for them to find new money for their organizations. The other 50 percent goes to organizations that may have spent ten years developing their programs between grants.

The third incentive is *leverage.* Some donors respond to the concept of bringing outside funding into the community. It may provide an incentive for the lead donors whose gifts are not being matched by the challenge grant but whose support is necessary for the application. And the donors whose gifts are made after the challenge grant might respond to the concept of extending their gifts on a one-to-three ratio, as is usually suggested. Thus, the leverage incentive helps the solicitor confidently invite new donors.

Finally, the challenge grant helps create a *meaningful deadline* for the campaign. As already noted, the last dollars in a campaign are the most difficult to raise. If the organization is to claim the challenge grant, the staff, volunteers, and prospective donors on the campaign committee realize they must meet the deadline. This helps motivate the staff and volunteers and prods to action those donors who are hesitating. No one wants to be the one responsible for sending the challenge grant back. The challenge grant inserts "creative anxiety" into a campaign. But these are factors that can be managed at the outset. The timing, the deadline, and the amount can all be strategically planned ahead of the campaign. The challenge grant should introduce the right challenge at the right time. The Kresge challenge grant will never be the reason for a campaign, but it can contribute to the campaign's success. It can be a catalyst, a change agent in the middle of a campaign.

Planning incentives

The Kresge application process also focuses the organization on its planning process. Applicants must focus on why they are building or renovating a facility or adding equipment in the first place. These capital improvements are not ends in themselves. How will programs be enhanced by the capital improvements? How can these programs be sustained after the capital campaign?

These questions focus the campaign on the organization's mission and the programs that result from it. They draw the talents of staff and board members into the planning process. The process creates investment or ownership among key leadership and may draw others in as well. The challenge grant application requires a feasibility study to determine a legitimate campaign goal and time frame. For some organizations this may be a first-time activity because they have had no previous campaign or because a single donor dominated the previous campaign. The planning process does not guarantee success, but it does enhance the possibility of success (Dove, 1988, p. 5; Rosso, 1991, p. 81).

The planning process for the grant application has a significant impact on the staff, board, and volunteers. Boards realize that they must expand their constituency, go out into the community in search of a broader base of involvement. They begin defining new geographic boundaries and new communities of interest. Their investment in the mission through the planning process also helps them become more than simply fundraisers but also witnesses to an important cause.

The Kresge challenge grant program is successful because it focuses planning for the capital campaign on programs related to the mission and the sustainability of those programs through an expanded donor base. The new capital developed in a campaign becomes a means to mission and program development, not an end in itself.

Some successes, some examples

One of the most successful Kresge grants was made to a museum that specialized in armor. Although the collection was highly rated, the organization did not have a suitable facility for bringing it to the public and developing its educational programs. The museum needed a renovated facility and a reinstallation. It had never conducted a capital campaign. When the volunteer campaign chair suggested to the consultant planning the campaign that the organization apply for a Kresge challenge grant, the consultant's response was that the organization did not have the stature to attract Kresge support.

The persistent CEO prepared an application for Kresge herself. A number of issues needed to be clarified and the application process forced some organizational planning. But the grant was ultimately made. The CEO wrote to Kresge, "When I received your letter and opened it, I had to run outside and scream." The grant had inspired and motivated the campaign chair, who achieved unimaginable results. In this case as in most others, the success of the challenge grant went far beyond the capital project. It provided the space for improved programs, enhanced the general fund to ensure sustainability, raised the image of the organization in the community, and helped increase the level of professionalism among the staff and board. That the organization was able to seek out The Kresge Foundation and complete the application process represented a success in itself. The board accepted the full range of its responsibilities and grew in its stewardship and involvement. The challenge grant application was a catalyst for the organization to address issues it might not otherwise have addressed.

Of course, there are sometimes failures. In the foundation's most disappointing year, 4 of the 175 grants awarded were canceled. There are a number of reasons for failure. Sometimes the grant has experimented with new approaches. For example, one grantee developed a plan to run the campaign in reverse order, soliciting the smaller gifts first to build confidence, then approaching corporations and soliciting major individual gifts last, based on the other support. The second phase did not work. Still, the organization did raise money from new donors even though it did not receive the challenge grant.

Sometimes the project may change in midstream. Although the application process encourages organizations to give details that are fairly final, unanticipated problems or redesigns sometimes drive up costs and extend the time frame past the deadline. Many problems have arisen when there is a change in leadership, which often extends the campaign beyond the deadline. In a few instances the campaigns have come to a complete stop.

Sometimes Kresge has accepted too much risk. Although it tries to make certain that the challenge grant is going to viable organizations, on occasion some have been too new or too grassroots— that is, too community-based—to draw in the support envisioned. At other times, the campaign has been put on hold to save the agency from operating budget misfortunes.

Other challenge grant successes
Capital campaigns that include endowment-building efforts should note that The Kresge Foundation, Lilly Endowment Inc., W. K. Kellogg Foundation, and others have successfully

challenged organizations and community foundations to raise significant endowment funds. With a mix of matches (some $1 for $2, others $1 for $1), Lilly Endowment has committed some $192 million to help create and endow community foundations in Indiana since 1990. Through September 1998, the endowment paid out nearly $88 million of that commitment, while the number of Indiana community foundations mushroomed from eleven functioning in 1990 to ninety-three in 1998 and their combined asset base grew from about $100 million to more than $600 million.

The Van Dusen Endowment Challenge, issued by the Kresge Foundation, was named for one of its trustees, a noted civic leader in Detroit. The goal was to establish a tradition of giving through the Community Foundation for Southeastern Michigan in Detroit. With a one-for-three match, the Van Dusen grants challenged nonprofit organizations to develop designated agency endowments in the Community Foundation. The organization had to have raised 10 percent of the total proposed in the application. Fifty percent of the applicants had no endowment, 80 percent had less than $250,000. The effort raised $50 million, including the match. Investment performance added another $15 million during the six years of the program as pledges were paid in. Kresge learned that one of the key obstacles to building an endowment was not having an endowment to begin with and thus not understanding what it could mean to an organization. So Kresge began paying 5 percent of the goal to the organization while the money was being raised. The realization of what the endowment could accomplish helped keep the organization motivated.

Conclusion

We believe that funders and donors should be encouraged to use challenge grants to assist organizations in planning and completing capital campaigns. The challenge grant strategy can be most helpful when it is integrated into the overall campaign and therefore does not become a distraction. The challenge grant donor should not become the focus of attention. People do not necessarily contribute to honor or please the challenging donor. A "phased challenge" can help keep the campaign moving if it is tied to achieving certain goals at certain times, but it needs to be kept simple or it can become a burden to smaller organizations. As this chapter noted, using the challenge grant near the end of a campaign has the added advantage of aiding the campaign during its most difficult period. However, several funders and donors interested in a campaign might consider joining forces to create a larger challenge or different challenges at different times in the campaign.

An organization seeking a challenge for its campaign from among its donor base must choose the donor carefully. The organization's other donors and new donors that the organization may want to involve must respect the challenge donor.

We believe that challenge grants can provide great incentives to both capital and endowment campaigns, as the examples described in this chapter illustrate. A challenge grant is an effective strategy for completing a campaign. However, it can also focus the institution on other positive outcomes of a campaign. Donors that make challenge grants should consider incentives to help the organization focus on defining its mission, planning for future programs and their sustainability, involving new constituencies, and raising the image of the organization in the community. Challenge grant funders and donors can also help engage and energize campaign leadership as well as provide a source of energy and inspiration during the last third of the campaign, a point when many campaigns lag. Finally, they can help set real deadlines for completing the campaign.

If focused on these goals, challenge grants can assist organizations to succeed in a way that goes far beyond the traditional goals of a new facility or the latest equipment. By disciplining organizations to plan well and broaden their donor bases, these grants can have far more lasting effects.

34   CAPITAL CAMPAIGNS

References

Dove, K. E. *Conducting a Successful Capital Campaign: A Comprehensive Fundraising Guide for Nonprofit Organizations.* San Francisco: Jossey-Bass, 1988.
The Fund Raising School. *Principles and Techniques of Fund Raising.* Section IV. Indianapolis: Indiana University Center on Philanthropy, 1998.
Kihlstedt, A., and Schwartz, C. P. *Capital Campaigns: Strategies That Work.* Gaithersburg, Md.: Aspen, 1997.
The Kresge Foundation. *Policies and Application Procedures.* Troy, Mich.: The Kresge Foundation, 1993.
Rosso, H. A. *Achieving Excellence in Fund Raising: A Comprehensive Guide to Principles, Strategies, and Methods.* San Francisco: Jossey-Bass, 1991.

JOHN E. MARSHALL III *has served in positions relating to philanthropy for twenty-eight years, including associate director of development at Brown University, executive director of The Rhode Island Foundation, and president and CEO of The Kresge Foundation.*

EUGENE R. TEMPEL *is executive director of the Indiana University Center on Philanthropy at Indiana University–Purdue University Indianapolis. He is professor of higher education and philanthropic studies and an author and presenter in philanthropic studies, nonprofit and fundraising management, and ethics.*

Leadership gifts are often the result of meaningful, long-term relationships with important donors. During a capital campaign, organizations can create the right conditions for leadership gifts to be made.

3

Achieving leadership gifts: The investment returns of lasting relationships

Rodney P. Kirsch, Martin W. Shell

IN JULY 1995, Osceola McCarty, a little-known, modest eighty-seven-year-old African American woman who had spent a lifetime washing and ironing other people's clothes, attracted national attention when she contributed $150,000—essentially her life's savings—to the University of Southern Mississippi in her hometown of Hattiesburg (Wertz, 1995).

Two years later, Ted Turner, the multibillionaire media mogul known throughout the world, pledged $1 billion to the United Nations—estimated to be slightly less than half of his worth (Fineman, 1997).

In 1997–98, the authors' own organizations each received the largest gifts from individuals in their histories—respectively, a commitment of $30 million from Bill and Joan Schreyer to endow an honors college at The Pennsylvania State University (Honon, 1997) and a gift of $15 million to the University of Pennsylvania Law School from Henry Silverman (O'Neill, 1998).

NEW DIRECTIONS FOR PHILANTHROPIC FUNDRAISING, NO. 21, FALL 1998 © JOSSEY-BASS PUBLISHERS

What compels such acts of philanthropy? What if anything do Ms. McCarty, Mr. Turner, the Schreyers, Mr. Silverman, and others have in common? How do inspirational leadership gifts like this come to pass? Even more importantly, what environmental conditions need to be present to influence such gifts, and what role do volunteers and professionals play in relationships to make such investments possible?

In 1996, $150.7 billion was contributed to American charities. The great majority of this—87 cents of each dollar—came from living individuals or through bequests. *Giving USA 1997* (p. 184) lists over three hundred gifts of $1 million or greater given by individuals to every part of the nonprofit-sector rainbow—religion, education, health, human services, the arts, the environment, and more. Many of these gifts come as leadership gifts to capital campaigns. This chapter focuses on the conditions necessary to achieve leadership investments from individuals, the role that institutional representatives play as catalysts in facilitating the right environment for leadership gifts, and how to position and utilize the positive dynamics created by such magnificent investments.

As the title indicates, such important acts of philanthropy are indeed *investments* that occur as the result of deep and meaningful *relationships* that span the course of *time*. They are as much "given" as they are "solicited." In this respect, they represent the convergence of factors that go well beyond the mechanics normally discussed in writings about soliciting large gifts, especially during campaigns.

This chapter also raises some cautions and considerations about how all fundraisers work in achieving lead gifts in the campaign context—considerations that take into account the many personal complexities in the lives of donors.

Defining a leadership gift

There are now more than six hundred thousand 501(c)3 organizations registered with the Internal Revenue Service as charities (*Giving USA 1997*, p. 59). The majority of them will not see a donor to their charity listed in the *Forbes* annual roster of largest gifts. This is not terribly important. What matters is that each of these charities can indeed achieve success with leadership commitments measured not simply by its past fundraising success but rather by the extraordinary potential each has to effect some change in the community it serves.

But before considering the optimal conditions for inspiring leadership gifts, it is best to define such gifts.

An inspirational gift

Lead gifts and the donors who make them possess transformational qualities. In other words, the impact of these gifts is to move an entire organization or a significant programmatic part of an organization forward in a single quantum leap. They create synergy for further philanthropy and define to the entire constituency the importance and value one donor holds for the organization. As one donor said recently about a lead gift, "It puts you on the map. Others will now more carefully consider the important contributions your organization makes."

Indeed, as the name implies, these gifts set a standard of leadership not only beyond what the organization might have achieved to date but also beyond what those close to the organization even thought possible. In many cases, it is not too bold to say that the most valuable lead gifts are truly *historic* in nature and can create a new chapter in the life of a charity.

These are philosophical and inspirational definitions of a lead gift and we encourage readers to consider these gifts in this manner. These are the kinds of investments to have in mind as you further consider this topic. There are, of course, more specific and concrete ways to define leadership gifts in a campaign environment, and alternative definitions are offered, but be aware that a strict definition in some cases may *lower* your donors' expectations and sights, rather than *raise* them to what might be possible if you and they venture truly to dream big dreams.

A portion of a donor's wealth

Unlike the examples of Ms. McCarty and Mr. Turner, the public normally does not know exactly what portion of a donor's entire wealth a gift may represent. Many times, the "professionals" do not know either. Certainly a gift that represents 20 percent or more of an individual's net worth would be considered substantive by most professional development officers and volunteers. But it may also be asked—notwithstanding the sheer difference in size of the gift—who sacrificed more, who made the bolder statement, Ms. McCarty or Mr. Turner? In the dynamic of campaigns, as gifts are awarded, those close to the organization—key volunteers, donors, and staff— at least have a feel for how sacrificial they are and, if they are wise, can and should use this knowledge to influence others discreetly and strategically.

Relationship to other large gifts

Another traditional way to define lead gifts is where they fit in relation to other major gifts in the life of a campaign. In this context, being among the top 2 or 3 percent of the largest gifts given would normally qualify a gift for this type of recognition. However, we offer some caution here. This definition is based on a relative comparison with others, not necessarily on what might represent the true potential of the donor or the kind of gift that fits the earlier philosophical definition.

A threshold amount

Perhaps the most conventional method of defining a lead gift is by its amount. This again will vary from organization to organization. For multimillion dollar campaigns, the figure may be $1 million. For more modest campaigns in organizations without a major gift culture, it may be $100,000 or $50,000. The danger with such an exact definition is what it does in limiting potential or possibly even lowering the sights among donors! Donors may meet only the minimum expected in the leadership category when in all likelihood there is potential to reach beyond this arbitrary level. A donor capable of $5 million may likely feel quite accomplished by committing a $1 million gift if that is the threshold set for leadership gifts.

Creating a leadership gift environment

Development professionals occupy a very privileged position in an American society that values philanthropy like no other nation in the world. Fundraisers have a great responsibility to serve their organizations and, through them, their immediate communities and the world beyond. They are in unique positions to link organizational problem-solving abilities to individuals (donors) who have an inherent desire to help solve the challenges of society. But before we explore the role fundraisers have as catalysts in this human drama, how to create the environment that fosters leadership gifts merits attention.

Shared purpose and passion

A leadership gift usually grows out of a close association between a donor and an organization based on a deeply held and mutually shared vision, belief, or value. At first blush this suggests that attention be paid to creating persuasive case statements and program brochures. But these standard campaign vehicles are only initial and, at best, superficial instruments on the road to inspiring leadership giving.

Each nonprofit organization should consider the constituencies it serves, the mission it holds dear, and the values it expresses when engaging individuals in the leadership gift process. The nonprofit's ability to articulate these important dimensions of its existence is an essential part of fostering an environment for leadership gift possibilities.

Experienced development professionals know from both surveys and personal anecdotal evidence that major philanthropy at its core is primarily based on emotion. This is particularly true of leadership gifts. Many individuals, often without much forethought, write checks every day for modest amounts of money to what they see as "a good cause." But major gifts—the kind that transform an organization—are usually tied to deeply held beliefs about the purpose of the nonprofit and are given with passion. Yes, the donor expects accountability after the gift is made, and surely tax implications are thoroughly examined during the gift decision-making stage. But the impulse causing a donor to consult her financial adviser or be concerned over the measurable outcomes from a leadership gift stems from her strong conviction about the work and purpose of the organization. This kind of passion cannot be evoked through brochures or annual reports, which over time have tended to make nonprofits look more alike than different to donors.

Instead, donors become passionate about an organization's purpose though genuine involvement in the organization's life. Thus, developing meaningful and personal relationships with prospects and donors is the primary theme of this chapter.

The most successful nonprofits find myriad ways to bring individual donors *inside* the organization, where they can help shape policy, test their values and interests against those of the organization, fully understand the mission as well as appreciate the impact of the organization, and ultimately discover the right channel to express their passion for the organization's work through philanthropy. Involvement of this type indeed begets investment. Nonprofits have the ability to choose just how and with whom they wish to encourage this special level of involvement. It should be done with the understanding that practical considerations like time constraints, governing structures, budgetary limitations, and program activities permit precious few individuals to see each organization in a unique and special way. Choose these individuals carefully. They will be the keys to discovering leadership donors for you, they will make those investments themselves, or both.

Genuine volunteer involvement

In recent times and in modern campaigns, the role of volunteers has diminished as staff have become more central to the process of securing leadership gifts. What has caused this shift and what are the consequences? First, nonprofit organizations have proliferated in the last twenty years. Today's donors say: "Everyone is raising money for something nowadays." That is true. As the nonprofit sector expands, there may indeed be fewer *good* volunteers to go around to meet current challenges. Even if one argues that there are as many good volunteers today, there are clearly more worthy causes and campaigns to be served. The economics of supply and demand have caused some organizations to deemphasize the role of volunteers.

Second, the growing ambitions of both new and well-established nonprofits has led organizations to seek full-time development officers where none existed previously. *The Chronicle of Philanthropy* is filled with ads that read, "This is a newly created position," or "This is a new position created to enhance the campaign staff." Full-time "professionals" are now serving where once volunteers did the work, or at least part of the work.

Third, as our philanthropic work becomes increasingly complex and the necessity to succeed becomes imperative, some organizations are deciding, consciously or not, that the work is too important and the risks are too high to let volunteers "interfere." They are simply not trusted, or it is felt that they are inadequately trained, insufficiently positioned, or improperly experienced to be sent out on such essential institutional missions. The litany behind such fears sounds something like this: "Volunteers take a lot of time to staff." "We will lose control of our programs." "They will misdirect us." "They don't really know the case for support." "Volunteers really aren't skilled solicitors." Nearly all development professionals at one time or another have had one or more of these concerns. Skillful staff can influence and overcome both the real and the imagined concerns so often expressed about volunteer involvement.

If volunteers are involved in campaigns, that involvement is often peripheral to the process of fundraising. In addition to asking them to make introductions and open doors, we feed them nice meals, give them fancy reports that share only good news, and let them rub elbows for a day or so every few months with their peers. The involvement is superficial at best. Not much is expected of them. In such cases, the results usually meet the expectations— not much time, advice, or resources are contributed to advance our organizations.

In modern and increasingly complex campaigns, well-selected, thoroughly educated, and genuinely enthusiastic volunteers who are true partners will become more, rather than less, critical when leadership gifts are sought. Paid development staff, no matter what type of nonprofit, can *never* substitute for effective volunteers who are genuinely involved with the organization. Recently, during a call on a prospect, a volunteer solicitor explained in moving terms how and why she and her husband had increased their gift five times beyond their original generous intention. This made a powerful impact on the prospect. Yes, there was a bit of stumbling on the volunteer's part to make the point. It wasn't perfectly scripted, but this type of heartfelt, spontaneous testimonial is simply irreplaceable. In fact, the mere presence of a volunteer at a solicitation call can make all the difference in the world. If nothing else, it shows the prospect that "I care, I took the time to be here."

The concern about the availability of good volunteers is legitimate. For this reason, it is more important than ever to seek aggressively their enhanced involvement rather than go it alone because they are too much trouble or unavailable. Remember, volunteers are more valuable than major gift prospects. Good volunteers are fewer in number and will affect organizations in multiple ways beyond just making a gift. Those organizations that meaningfully incorporate volunteers in their campaign structure will add immeasurably to an environment conducive to leadership gifts. Organizations that seek genuine volunteer involvement offer proper orientation, personalized staffing, and shared planning and decision making, and they respect honest differences of opinion. They make conscious decisions about the selection of *each* volunteer for *every* role these institutions envision. They commit to peer-to-peer personal recruitment done in the same thoughtful fashion as solicitation. And they take into consideration that time is often more valuable to key volunteers than money. The active participation of volunteers in guiding case statement development, strategizing on others' involvement, providing peer influence and leverage on solicitation calls—all lead to effective leadership gift achievement.

Finally, before leaving the topic of meaningfully engaging volunteers, it is important to underscore a cardinal rule of fundraising, particularly when it comes to leadership gifts: *Volunteers must also be donors. This rule should never be violated.* A volunteer who has not given is less effective than staff and sometimes even damaging to an organization wishing to build its philanthropic culture. An important corollary to this principle is expressed by our consultant friend John Glier, president and CEO of Grenzebach, Glier and Associates, who advises to recruit and solicit volunteers at the same time. There may be cases when this is not practical, but the intent is clear. Effective and authentic volunteers support generously the causes to which they give their time.

Mature, ongoing relationships

How many times have you personally been named a beneficiary in a will from someone unknown to you? In the same vein, leadership gifts from strangers are wonderful but exceedingly rare. Leadership gifts invariably come from individuals who have known an organization for a long time.

Endeavor daily to develop ever-deepening relationships with your key stakeholders. The process of genuine engagement with volunteers is one that must be extended to a broader circle of interested parties. This is a process of selection, one where the donor selects you and you select the donor for a long-term or even a lifetime relationship.

One of the most critical errors made in securing leadership gifts is failing to look beyond the immediate campaign to what James Gregory Lord, noted fundraising consultant and author of *The Raising of Money*, urged professionals to consider during a seminar many years ago: the lifetime value of a donor's relationship with your organization. The donor's timetable versus the organization's is discussed in a later section, but the concept of the lifelong relationship and the attitude of valuing lifetime friendships with donors is central to creating an environment for leadership gifts.

When you think about your relationships with your volunteers, donors, and other stakeholders over the long term, several fundamental ideas come into focus. First, *quality is more important than quantity.* Creating a positive climate for leadership giving, within and outside the campaign context, is not a mass-production, assembly-line process. As our colleague Kent Dove, author of *Conducting a Successful Capital Campaign,* notes, "Wealth is not democratically distributed in our society." Indeed, half of 1 percent of the population owns 27 percent of the wealth in the United States. The top 10 percent of the population owns 68 percent of the nation's wealth ("Focus On," 1997). We are best served if we focus our time on building mature relationships with individuals who can ultimately make the kind of impact gifts described earlier. This need not be a cold and calculating activity. Indeed, your role is to serve as a catalyst in these relationships, a topic more fully discussed in the next section. Facilitating these relationships is both a rewarding and a consuming process. It is a time-intensive but worthy investment. It is more essential than ever to focus attention on building quality relationships with fewer individuals rather than to seek many relationships that never go beyond a superficial level.

Second, *multiple relationships within the organization add value.* The best volunteers and most generous donors are those who extend their involvement in multiple ways. Over time they may serve on different committees, contribute to different programs within your organization, and have numerous personal relationships, extending from the CEO to clients served by the nonprofit. Several years ago, one institution discovered that a leadership prospect to a large organization had directed gifts of modest size over time to nearly twenty separate purposes within the organization. Needless to say, this donor had established multiple interests and many personal relationships at different levels of the organization. These relationships contributed to a deeper understanding of the organization's mission and the broad impact the organization had on its constituency. When it came time to make a multimillion-dollar leadership investment to a singular program, there is no doubt that these previous multiple relationships played a role in the donor's continuing interest in and willingness to make a transformational gift—which he did at a level of more than $20 million.

In organizations large and small, the focus should be on managing and, when appropriate, even creating multiple relationships inside the organization. Too often the first instinct is to direct the prospect to a "priority program" rather than allow the individual to explore his or her own interests. Organizations should encourage multiple contacts and connections rather than restrict them.

Third, *past donors are most likely to be future investors.* Treat them well. There is nothing more fundamental than remembering to remember past and current donors. During a consultation visit, a college president complained that his staff relied too heavily on the "Casablanca method" of fundraising—"rounding up the usual suspects," as he put it, rather than broadening the donor base. Surely, every nonprofit organization must find new friends if it is to keep vibrant and move forward. However, it is in carefully stewarding relationships with past and current donors that an environment conducive to leadership gifts will evolve. If nonprofits candidly examine where they place their priorities, most would discover that they are much busier looking for the next big prospect than stewarding the last major donor. This is a mistake. Stewardship activities are discussed more fully in the next section, but it should be mentioned here that the challenge for those in the nonprofit sector is to focus as much energy on stewardship as on solicitation, thus creating an appropriately balanced environment for continuous leadership giving.

The chief staff person

The role of the chief staff person in the campaign—particularly when it comes to securing leadership gifts—has only increased in importance over time. (For purposes of discussion, the chief staff person may carry any number of different titles—executive director, president, headmaster, superintendent, chief executive officer, and all the rest. The intent is to focus on the top individual staff person who holds overall responsibility for the nonprofit organization. We will hereafter refer to this person as the CEO.) Today's nonprofits are increasingly complex and sophisticated. How well they are led and managed influences leadership giving, particularly during a capital campaign when the organization is subject to increased external scrutiny. Donors are more discerning than ever when selecting the recipients of their philanthropy. They are also more demanding about organizational performance and account-ability. It is one thing for donors to *feel* good about an organization, that is, for an organization to evoke emotion and loyalty from supporters. It is another thing entirely for an organization to demonstrate to a donor that it *is* good in carrying out its nonprofit mission and be able to prove it. Much of this responsibility resides with the CEO.

The CEO's role is multifaceted. Most of a CEO's actions and decisions can influence positively or negatively the relationships the organization has with donors. The CEO creates a vision (ide-ally, in tandem with other partners, most notably the board) for the organization. She sets forth a strategic direction, often deciding which programs or services will or will not be pursued. She holds responsibility for the financial welfare of the organization and makes key decisions in selecting other top-level staff. And finally, among many other duties, she acts as the chief public relations per-son, the spokesperson in all important matters related to the non-profit. It is for these reasons and others that the relationship between the CEO and key stakeholders (that is, leadership prospects) takes on a special, vital, defining dimension.

Just as no staff person can substitute fully for a volunteer when it comes to solicitation, so too no one can substitute for the CEO when it comes to developing personal relationships with key lead-ership gift individuals. Most significant leadership donors truly care about the organizations they support. They yearn to have a close, insider's relationship, a "place at the table." They want to have a finger on the pulse of the organization, know its challenges as well as its triumphs, share in its governance and future direc-tion, have their opinions taken seriously. The best way for them to gain this insight, satisfy this curiosity, and be reassured that their investment of time and money is well-spent is through a close personal relationship with the CEO. It is fundamental to the leadership gift process that outsiders be made into insiders.

Involvement begets investment. Strategic involvement begets leadership investment.

And if leadership givers see themselves as "buying equity" in the organization, then the CEO is the chief equity manager. Donors seldom make large philanthropic investments without some knowledge of and personal relationship with the CEO. If you expect to enhance your potential to secure leadership gifts, then the CEO's intellectual, emotional, and physical commitment to relationship building at a personal one-on-one level with top volunteers and donors is absolutely critical. Here again, quality is more important than quantity.

The act of asking

In April 1998, Joan and Sanford Weill announced a gift of $100 million to name Cornell University's medical center (Arenson, 1998). When asked during a press conference how they had decided to make this gift, Sanford Weill pointed to Cornell's president and medical dean and said, "They asked." Although circumstances surrounding this gift are private, it can probably be surmised that it was not quite so simple. Yet Weill's brief and spontaneous answer is poignant. It teaches once again the age-old lesson of fundraising at any level: the single largest mistake that is made in major gift fundraising is to fail to ask for the gift. Consequently, the most important thing to do in major gift solicitation is to ask for the gift.

As the key conditions for lead gifts are refined, the act of asking, although it seems obvious, cannot be taken for granted. How many lead gifts have never materialized because a request was not forthcoming, even though all the other factors were in place? How many lead gifts went to "another organization" because that nonprofit group made the request? How many gifts never reached their full potential because the strategy was based on insufficient thought and little homework?

The intention here is not to list the elements of a successful solicitation call or provide stock answers to typical objections encountered in such meetings. Rather, it is to underscore the significance of *actively, directly, and aggressively* seeking philanthropic investments of the highest possible magnitude. If the proper steps are taken to develop an environment and culture conducive to leadership giving, then achieving a significant gift commitment will follow naturally.

Exploration of donor values, presence of mature relationships, volunteer engagement, personal involvement by the organization's top leader—all of these factors and more become part of getting a donor ready to say "Yes" to a direct proposal or to ask "How much will it take?" when a vision requiring a philanthropic investment is presented. Of course, none of this can happen without a firm commitment on the part of an organization to sustained and focused volunteer and donor contact.

All leadership gift solicitations are unique. Each prospect is a minicampaign requiring specialized attention, creative approaches, and a solicitation grounded in the right strategy. Leadership solicitation is no more than choosing the right volunteer to ask the right prospect for the right purpose in the right amount at the right time in the right way. The solution to these key elements is not found in a vacuum, but rather through quality interaction with our volunteers, prospects, and donors.

Establishing leadership gift solicitation strategies requires a significant investment of time by the nonprofit organization. The process we describe here is labor-intensive and very personalized. Devoting ample budgetary resources to it is essential. Budgetary investments in a campaign that lead to enhanced direct contact with the prospect will have the greatest impact on leadership giving.

One other element involved in the act of asking bears emphasis: *challenge the donor*, both by amount and by purpose. Stay within the bounds of reason and good professional judgment, certainly, but challenge the donor's competitive spirit to stretch, not just financially but intellectually and emotionally as well. The most emotionally and intellectually committed leadership gift prospects will expect nonprofit organizations to present them with concepts that respond to their own strong impulses to transform organizations through philanthropy.

The role of institutional representatives: Catalysts behind lead gifts

After examining the role and importance that volunteers and the chief executive officer have in securing a successful leadership gift, we must now turn to the professional staff person—the facilitator who, through perseverance, patience, practice, and persuasion, brings together the elements that result in transformational gifts. In many ways, the professional advancement staff is the glue that holds together the lead gift process.

Staffing the chief executive officer

One of the advancement officer's most important roles is staffing the CEO. The CEO is paramount in most transformational gifts. He usually is an organization's best fundraiser but, as indicated earlier, has many responsibilities in addition to fundraising. There are unlimited demands on a CEO's limited time. Therefore, it is the advancement officer's responsibility to ensure that the leadership gift activity is managed effectively and that the CEO's time is judiciously used in advancing the institution.

This can be a challenging task. If effective, however, advancement professionals can make extraordinary contributions to their institutions. John Glier encourages development officers to "manage" the CEO much as volunteers and key donors are managed. That suggestion can be helpful in preparing the CEO for advancement work. Thinking of the CEO as our most important volunteer causes us to be much more thorough with the information, level of staffing, and strategies we develop on top prospects.

Effective staffing of the CEO, however, goes well beyond what is needed for a specific call or prospect. In the most successful cases, the advancement officer develops a close, comfortable working relationship with the CEO. Development officers often spend great amounts of time with the CEO. Colin Diver, dean of the University of Pennsylvania Law School, notes, "I spend more time with my chief development officer than anyone other than my wife" (personal communication). Fundraisers *do* spend a lot of time with their CEOs (or at least they should during campaigns), and often for long stretches in less than idyllic circumstances. Waiting in San Francisco for the rain-delayed shuttle two days before Thanksgiving will not make the travel highlights film. In such circumstances it helps immensely if the CEO and the advancement officer respect and are compatible with each other. It helps, but it is not an absolute requirement.

Another extremely helpful tool in the CEO–development officer relationship is humor. Ours is an inexact profession, populated by imperfect humans, working with other humans whose imperfections routinely reveal themselves. Laughing at our own and other's foibles helps make those long trips and difficult calls much easier. Humor can also be a good vehicle to help communicate why things did not work and how they might be improved. Humor helps build stronger relationships with our CEOs and key volunteers—it reveals our humanity, forging a stronger relationship with these individuals. Fundraisers are in the relationship business, and some of the most important relationships are with our CEOs and key volunteers.

Complementary work

When working with the CEO or a volunteer, the advancement professional should be the complementing factor. When accompanying the CEO on a visit or during the cultivation process, the role is to complement. The Latin root of complement means *that which fills up or completes*. In most cases, the advancement professional's role is secondary—completing—whereas the CEO or volunteer has the primary responsibility. Most lead donors expect the CEO or volunteer to be the primary point person. But although it may be secondary, the fundraiser's role is vital.

Professional staff become the eyes, ears, and engine of the cultivation process. The role is to think strategically and creatively about strengthening the stakeholder's ties to the institution. This requires focusing on the donor's needs, wants, and desires, and then matching them with the mission, purposes, and requirements of the institution. Fundraisers must know both the donor and the institution very well. The opportunities for interaction between benefactors and institutions are countless, and professional staff must be creative and productive in finding opportunities to bring them together. The cultivation "mechanics" may be as simple as having a scholarship recipient write a note of thanks to the person who made the gift possible. It may be as elaborate as scheduling a symposium focused solely on the donor's life, work, and contributions to society. The limitations are individual creativity, time, institutional resources, and other demands on schedules.

The act of listening

It is the advancement officer's responsibility to make these cultivation mechanics happen, which requires an often underemployed skill—listening. *Advancement listening*, a term not normally found in books on listening skills, requires us to develop a very keen sense of what a donor is and is not saying.

This kind of listening may be illustrated by an extremely committed donor and volunteer. His relationship had followed the classic development track: initial identification, development officer visit, then a strong relationship with the CEO. The donor now is a member of the institution's board. Throughout this process, the donor's giving increased. When the CEO began talking about a leadership-level gift, he stressed the need to grow the institution's endowment. The donor listened intently each time the subject was raised but kept turning the conversation to a specific building project that also was on the drawing board. The building project was important, but it was not the institution's highest priority. After repeated conversations, the advancement officer and the CEO decided they should listen to the donor. That active listening netted a $2 million building gift with tremendous potential for more. This gift now has become the donor's single largest gift ever by a factor of ten.

Again, the building project was important to the institution but not the CEO's highest priority. It was a project, however, that would be needed to be done within a five-year period. Therefore, it had long-term importance to the institution and could, if successfully stewarded, generate even greater investment by the volunteer. This is the kind of lifetime value that James Gregory Lord speaks about. The CEO chose to subordinate his priorities to help match the donor's interest with a worthy but less immediate project. That decision will likely net the institution millions of additional gift dollars in the years ahead. The next leadership gift from the donor likely will be for endowment purposes.

Not every case of active listening ends as positively. There are cases when an institution must retreat from a gift discussion because the donor's wishes are not compatible with the institution's needs. Such cases are examples of the unique relationship between donors and institutions. Although donors make tremendous investments in organizations, they do not run them. The CEO and the institution's governing bodies determine which gifts are acceptable and for what purposes. They set the priorities for the organization. Fortunate is the institution that is not financially dependent on its next leadership gift. It is vital for any institution, regardless of its financial condition, to maintain integrity regarding the gifts it will and will not accept.

Stewardship

At most institutions, gift support is rarely turned away. A much larger challenge for advancement officers is the proper stewardship of gifts to our institutions.

There are several concepts about stewardship. The original concept predates the Bible but is codified in biblical language: all possessions belong to God and humanity is responsible for managing those resources while on earth. In feudal Europe, the steward was the person who ran the manor house, particularly the financial aspects of the estate. The green movement of the past few decades uses the concept to emphasize the need for all people to be stewards of the earth's natural resources. An underlying element in each definition is high morality and responsible management. A proper steward is one who is morally responsible and trustworthy.

Stewarding donors may not be seen as a moral obligation, but it is an important concept. Donors have chosen to invest in our institutions. They give time, energy, resources, and talent. As stewards of the manor, it is our responsibility to use those gifts wisely and account for those uses properly. Donors place great trust in nonprofit institutions. With this in mind, institutions should be systematic about telling their donors how their money is used. There should be immediate response to inquiries about how gifts and other assets are managed. Good stewardship also requires communicating with donors when institutional needs change and if those changes affect their gifts.

There are also extremely practical reasons for being good stewards. No reasonable person would continue sending money to a financial institution that failed to report regularly on the investment. If you want your most committed stakeholders to remain just that, you should be forthright and regular in reporting on the rich dividends their gifts are paying at your institutions.

Good stewardship leads quite naturally to strengthening existing relationships and building new ones within the organization. Donors are investors. They are interested in seeing "a return on their investment." The stewardship requirement for leadership prospects and donors goes far beyond an annual report on endowment performance or an annual visit from the organization's president. Good stewardship is a personal, carefully managed process. It aims not simply to keep a donor satisfied but to increase satisfaction to the point where the donor asks, "What more can I do?" Good stewardship is not the end of the solicitation cycle but the beginning of a new and higher level of donor involvement.

Positioning leadership gifts in a campaign context

When capital campaign goals crossed the billion-dollar mark in the late 1980s, some speculated that campaigns could not sustain themselves at such rarefied heights. But with the record-breaking bull market and growing worldwide wealth of the 1990s one now wonders if campaigns will ever end. Like the bunny made famous by the television commercials, campaigns keep going and going with higher and higher goals. Campaigns will remain part of the fundraising landscape for one simple reason: They work—they raise money.

In expressing this, leadership gifts have never been more important to today's campaigns. Transformational gifts represent huge percentages of campaign totals. Capital campaign goals continue growing at a feverish pace because leadership gifts too are escalating exponentially.

Do donors really care about goals and do campaigns provide an excuse to ask for unprecedented gifts? Twenty years ago donors might not have cared as much about the details of capital campaigns. Today, however, they often care deeply about whether their gift is made in a campaign context. Why?

The decision to make a campaign gift is not always related to the donor's desire to be included in a mass appeal for funds. Rather, it reflects the evolutionary role of campaigns and the programs those campaigns seek to fund. It also reflects the increased level of donor sophistication. Successful capital campaigns today are a direct outgrowth of an institution's strategic planning process. Institutional needs are not simply brought to the CEO's desk and converted into a campaign brochure. The needs, goals, ambitions, and mission of the institution should be debated, discussed, and determined. The campaign is an outgrowth of the institution's strategic thinking. Leadership donors increasingly want to know that their gifts will be used for specific strategic purposes. The Wharton School at the University of Pennsylvania announced in May 1998 the largest single gift to a business school in the United States. It was an unrestricted gift. The University of Pennsylvania Law School announced in February 1998 the largest outright gift to a law school for construction and endowment purposes. In both examples, the donors were key volunteers who had some hand in shaping institutional direction and ambition.

Involving key volunteers and donors in strategic planning also is vital to a campaign's success. Committed outsiders bring real-world perspective to the planning process. Furthermore, these donors become much more committed to the process and are more invested in its successful outcome when they have been consulted. Donors "cultivate themselves" if they become familiar with the strengths and needs of the institution. This is not to suggest that the planning process be turned over to the donors and volunteers. Institutional representatives ultimately must develop and implement a strategic plan. But involving key constituents will make it much easier to find resources when the time comes to fund the strategic initiatives. Donors do "care" about campaigns when the case for support has been clearly developed and can be backed by strategic analysis.

Capital campaigns provide a framework that makes it much easier to secure leadership gifts. That is because deadlines make decision making more efficient. Indeed, this chapter would still be but a glimmer in the authors' eyes had our editors not set a deadline. The same is true for donative decisions. Donors will be more efficient with their gift decisions when deadlines are set. Campaigns set deadlines, benchmarks, and goals.

The deadline concept is often refined further in campaigns. Most campaigns do not "go public" until a certain percent of the goal has been committed, usually between 40 and 60 percent. Leadership gifts represent the bulk of this lead money raised during the campaign's quiet phase. Asking lead donors to make their gift commitment early, before the campaign goes public, creates another deadline that can result in a gift decision. Skillful campaign leaders often set several minideadlines as a way to benchmark progress and help close gifts.

Capital campaigns also provide a bandwagon effect. Campaign-conditioned donors often expect to be a part of this effect. Some donors will not make a gift decision unless they know it is a part of a larger institutional fundraising effort. "I don't want to be a lone wolf," one donor said a few years ago. Leadership-level donors want their gifts to be a part of other large contributions. Campaigns provide that forum. This rising tide encourages others to join in. Donors want to associate themselves with successful organizations. Successful campaigns provide all that.

Campaigns also provide a formal structure for recognizing philanthropy, including regular stewardship and public relations opportunities such as donor recognition dinners, news releases, and periodic campaign updates. The campaign format increases the visibility of the donor's gift. It also provides a larger audience for these gifts. Gift announcements let institutions reinforce the campaign's overarching goals and highlight how the donor's investment supports the institutional mission. Donor recognition is an important part of the stewardship process because it is another way to thank the donor for a gift.

Of course, not every donor prefers this recognition. This was the situation recently when an institution received a very large gift—a record breaker—but both the gift and the donor's identity had to remain unknown. The donor did not want to make headlines with his philanthropy. This attitude is uncommon, and even refreshing, in our world of hype and advertising. However, the opportunity to take full advantage of peer-to-peer, leveraged, sight-raising philanthropy is lost in such situations.

In contrast, some important donors give for reasons other than simple altruism. Ego gratification often plays a very important role. A major donor may want regional and national publicity for his commitment. He may want peers and other volunteer leaders in the organization to know of his generosity and also want family and social colleagues to be aware of the gift. Major donors often have been highly successful in their business and professional lives and have developed strong competitive instincts. Indeed, that competitive spirit is often what makes them so successful. That same drive may motivate them to make a major gift or feel challenged to make an even larger commitment. Leadership gifts can be a vehicle through which these highly competitive, successful individuals, who often have equally well-developed egos, make a statement to the business and philanthropic worlds.

Such donors can and should be exacting about the publicity they receive for their gifts. Although organizations cannot guarantee media coverage of gift announcements, some donors expect as much. Capital campaigns often help in this area. They provide a context and a message for the gift announcement. The campaign messages give the media something else to report on in addition to the donor and the gift usage. A campaign also creates several follow-up opportunities to publicize donor gifts. Campaign publications are no substitute for prominent news coverage, but they do provide communication vehicles ensuring that your institution's message is delivered to the audience you choose at the time you wish.

An important consideration in announcing leadership gifts is the staging, sequencing, and pacing of these announcements during campaign events and meetings. This strategy can have a strong motivational impact on both internal and external audiences. If a donor couple personally announces their gift to peers, it has a tremendous emotional effect on those who have not yet given. These personal testimonies and the life stories behind them can be exemplary in raising the standard for the next cycle of campaign gifts.

A final word about press releases on gifts: Keep the donors well-informed. It is vital to stay in touch with them throughout the gift decision process, but it is equally important to keep them informed about the announcement strategies. It is better to err by giving the donor too many opportunities to change a news release or have input on the circumstances surrounding an announcement. Such inconveniences are preferable by far to dealing with an angry donor who has not felt properly consulted about a lead gift that, after all, is an extremely personal matter.

Other considerations

In addition to working with a donor or a donor couple, fundraisers often work with those associated with an individual donor, including spouses, significant others, children, other heirs, administrative staff, and financial and legal advisers. These individuals can play a crucial role in the gift decision process and subsequent stewardship activity. Our organizations benefit when development officers know when to involve people associated with the donor. These people may be either advocates or adversaries in the gift-giving process. So the best rule is to involve them as early as possible.

Family and heirs raise special issues when negotiating major gifts. They often have a personal stake in the commitment and believe they have a vested interest in the process. It is up to the development officer and sometimes the donor himself or herself to demonstrate that the gift decision is in the donor's best interest. Through creative planned gift vehicles, a development officer can help design a gift strategy that often benefits the donor, the donor's heirs, and the charitable organization.

Negotiations on these types of gift arrangements may involve the donor's financial and legal counsel. As development officers, we often validate the donor's gift intention to the advisers. This is especially true when an adviser is looking for reasons to stop the donor from making a gift. Development officers should have working knowledge of the financial and tax implications of charitable gifts or have quick access to people who do. Although most donors make leadership gifts for reasons other than tax and estate benefits, the tax laws provide real opportunities for charitably minded people. This has never been truer than with today's financial markets, where millions of potential new major donors have been created by the dramatic increase in the value of the equity markets. Gifts of appreciated securities today are becoming the currency of choice for major donors. Development professionals must be well-versed in the nuances of stock gifts. Some donors may make gift decisions when a stock reaches a specific value or may time the gift in conjunction with a capital event, like a company takeover or initial public offering.

Stock gifts in a donor's publicly traded corporation can also create special challenges and opportunities. High-profile executives or board members who use corporate stock as their gift vehicle often worry about adverse market reaction to their liquidation of stock for gift purposes. Some corporate insiders will not make significant stock gifts because they fear misinterpretation in the market of their intent to give away securities. In each circumstance, flexibility and creativity are required when working with donors and their advisers.

Most donors also take into consideration today's longer life expectancy and have concerns about maintaining a certain living standard. Most people are living longer than their parents did and many will remain much more active later in life and want to be able maintain their lifestyle. Longer life expectancy also may mean additional costs associated with long-term care of the individual or spouse or both. Such possibilities can create a tremendous demand on our donors to hold resources that otherwise might be given to our organizations. As development professionals we must work with them to craft gift arrangements that benefit both them and our organizations. The ethics of our profession require us to maintain a fiduciary relationship with our donors. There is an old fundraising saw that says, "No one will protect the donor's wallet like the donor." Still, life expectancy concerns are real and they must be treated respectfully and honestly as we work with our major donors, especially older ones.

Final thoughts

Successful capital campaigns today depend on our organizations' relationships with a small collection of very important people. These individuals represent the leadership and financial lifeblood of our institutions. They can literally hold the future of our organizations in their hands. Acts of tremendous philanthropy like that of Ted Turner or of incredible generosity and sacrifice like that of Osceola McCarty result when people are connected to the mission and opportunities inherent in every nonprofit organization. As development professionals, our challenge and our opportunity are to match them with our organization, creating the context in which gift proposals become transformational gifts.

The greatest joy and highest good in philanthropic work comes when development professionals move beyond the "mechanics of fundraising" and "sealing the deal." Greater success will be achieved if fundraisers have a long-term view about their work and if they understand that, for the most part, leadership investments are about building lasting relationships that offer meaning and value to the donor first and benefits to our organizations second. When the donor's interests and vision are placed before the organization's needs, the potential is unleashed to move organizations forward through philanthropy.

References

Arenson, K. W. "$100 Million Donation to Cornell for Medicine." *The New York Times,* May 1, 1998, p. A27.

Dove, K. E. *Conducting a Successful Capital Campaign.* San Francisco: Jossey-Bass, 1988.

Fineman, H. "Why Ted Gave It Away: In an Autumnal Mood, Ted Turner Springs a $1 Billion Gift on the United Nations." *Newsweek,* Sept. 29, 1997.

"Focus On: The Distribution of Wealth." Press release. [http://uaw.org/uawreleases/jobs_pay_economy/1097/stat1097_03.html] July 17, 1997.

Giving USA 1997. New York: American Association of Fund-Raising Counsel Trust for Philanthropy, 1997.

Honon, W. H. "Couple Gives $30 Million to Penn State." *The New York Times,* Sept. 15, 1997, p. 14.

Lord, J. G. *The Raising of Money: Thirty-Five Essentials Every Trustee Should Know.* Cleveland, Ohio: Third Sector Press, 1990.

O'Neill, J. M. "Big Gift for Law School at Penn." *Philadelphia Inquirer,* Feb. 26, 1998.

Wertz, S. "Osceola McCarty Donates $150,000 to USM." Press release. [http//www.dept.usm.edu] July 1, 1995.

RODNEY P. KIRSCH *is vice president for development and alumni relations at The Pennsylvania State University.*

MARTIN W. SHELL *is associate dean for external relations at Stanford Law School. He was assistant dean for development and alumni relations at the University of Pennsylvania Law School when this chapter was originally drafted.*

Setting realistic and challenging goals requires a link between fundraising potential and serious institutional planning, assessment of the institution's maturity and that of its fundraising efforts (not always the same thing), and hard-nosed analysis of the sources of support.

4

Campaign goals: Taking aim at a moving target

Robert Pierpont, G. Steven Wilkerson

SOME PEOPLE BELIEVE that goals limit an organization's potential or threaten their personal survival in the organization. In the worst cases, goals are set casually and outside the planning process. Development staff are especially vulnerable to poor goal setting, both those they set themselves and those imposed by management or boards. It is therefore essential that goal setting be approached seriously and systematically, preferably by a team composed of board leaders, institutional executives, and development officers. In some instances a consultant may be a helpful team member too.

Among the organization's leadership, the underlying problem to be dealt with is often stated something like this: "Let's find out what people want to give for and how much they will give." "We have no choice but to raise this if we are to survive!" "If you [the development office or officer] don't or can't raise this, you should look

NEW DIRECTIONS FOR PHILANTHROPIC FUNDRAISING, NO. 21, FALL 1998 © JOSSEY-BASS PUBLISHERS

for another job." "Next year we will be fifty. Let's have a $50 million goal and a big anniversary celebration." "We will do everything we can to raise as much as possible, and that will be determined by what we find out when we are working with prospects and donors, not by projections made abstractly in advance."

For other people, goals are the organizing device of life itself. Without goals, these people are lost. After all, what is the point of doing anything if not to accomplish something? Aren't we really pursuing a goal with everything we do, whether we know what it is or not? Some wag once said if you don't know where you're going, any road will get you there. Just as golfers strive to break par, a fundraising effort—and certainly anything called a campaign—must have a goal, objective, target, or other device to give it purpose and drive and permit monitoring and evaluation of dollars raised against a scheduled deadline.

We believe that goals are essential, for reasons growing from the truths embedded in the earlier comments. Knowing what people want to give to and how much they will give—to the extent that this can be known or projected—is important if the organization is to accomplish the purposes for which it needs the money. If the institution must have a certain sum to survive, then gaining as much knowledge as possible of the real dollar potential is certain to affect the strategy of the institution and the campaign. If the development program lacks the capability to raise the funds required, then it is essential to deal with that before setting a campaign goal if it is to have a chance to succeed. If the institution has no effective planning process to determine its needs and set out compelling reasons for meeting them, then such a process will have to be put in place in order for any goal to bear the scrutiny of thoughtful prospects. Although no goal's accomplishment will be unaffected by the reality it encounters, that fact is an argument for setting goals as thoughtfully as possible and monitoring performance closely to make intelligent changes on the basis of knowledge gained in progress. Plans can only be managed and adjusted to accommodate the unexpected when there is some agreed-upon target at the start.

Other reasons for setting goals carefully have to do with the future viability and fundraising capability of the organization:

- A goal set unrealistically high will not be met. Failure to achieve goals is debilitating to volunteer leadership (and often fatal to staff leadership) and can create a long-lasting feeling of institutional caution that can make it very difficult to generate enthusiasm for even a well-conceived future campaign.
- A goal set unrealistically low means unrealized potential both in prospects and in dollars, something most organizations cannot afford.

Challenging goals arrived at intelligently help ensure against either of these undesirable outcomes.

Of course, many times the goal is not a moving target. If a community center is to build a swimming pool and there is no other pool in town, the goal may be fairly obvious—the cost of a well-designed pool adequate to accommodate the anticipated demand for instruction, recreation, and competition. This chapter focuses on the more complex situations, where a goal may include funds for substantial physical plant improvements, new buildings, endowments to provide a revenue stream from earnings, and perhaps annual support that will be "counted" in the capital campaign. What counts is not an issue if the campaign goal is simply to meet architect fees, contractors' costs, and fundraising expenses that must be paid if there is to be a community pool. But it *is* an issue when the goal includes endowment or annual support. Usually, endowment and annual gifts count in comprehensive campaigns if they are for the campaign's objectives. (Those who wish to explore the complexities of score keeping in campaigns will find the best current thinking in *CASE Management Reporting Standards* [Council for Advancement and Support of Education, 1996, 1998]).

This chapter discusses two broad aspects of goal setting for capital campaigns: some of the difficulties that may be encountered, and the importance of institutional planning as the basis for goal setting, including the use of gift range tables and feasibility studies.

The role of development staff

Differences of opinion over goals are frequently a result of individual experiences with planning in an organization. The most frequent division arises as a result of excluding development and fundraising staff from participation in developing plans, usually on the basis that "they don't know anything about the substance, mission, culture, and values of the institution, they just know about getting money." In fact, the degree to which development professionals can contribute substance to the mission of the organization varies greatly. However, more importantly, this kind of argument misses the point of their involvement. The planning process will almost certainly reveal future opportunities and needs that exceed the organization's fundraising capacity in a three- or five-year campaign. Knowing the larger dimensions of the institution's ambitions and time horizon, the choices made among proposed priorities, and the anticipated dollar cost of the needs described, permits the case for support to be prepared thoughtfully and consistently, allows unforeseen opportunities for gifts to be examined thoughtfully, and allows campaign goals to be set to match institutional and prospect interests to secure the largest goals possible. Thus, leaving development staff out of the planning process is like passing the last gas station with a tank half full before beginning a desert crossing. Good luck. But there are other perspectives that are not so foolish.

The leader who wants to find out what organizational needs people will give to and who then goes after them is likely to be one who thinks that this is the way to maximize support for the organization, calculating that "more is better," whether the "more" goes exactly where it is most needed or simply meets a lesser need more fully. Launching campaigns before knowing if the objectives are those for which people will give seems at least misguided, if not downright dumb. Merely taking anything that comes your way can be fatal to achieving your plans.

The experienced development officer knows that "more is better" is not always the case. If the organizational mission and campaign objectives appeal to a very limited audience, and that audience includes few with the capacity to support it generously or influence others who can, the potential for failure is high.

When the goal is set automatically because the organization cannot survive without achieving it, there is usually no plan to follow and desperation is the strategy. Experienced development officers know that donors of significant sums rarely want to risk seeing their money spent on a failing enterprise. These donors have too many strong organizations appealing to them to risk investing large sums in an organization whose future is truly in question.

Goals set to threaten development officers are a reflection of leadership that does not understand the development process and has expectations that are likely to be unmet no matter how many development officers come and go. The potential for support is not initially related to the competence of the staff and without a compelling plan presented persuasively, the staff is disarmed, as is the organization.

There is nothing about an anniversary that makes a goal based on that number feasible. Cavalier treatment of organizational planning and fundraising efforts signals weaknesses more important than lack of money. The development officer stuck in this setting should be polishing his or her resume.

In each of these situations, the focus is on fundraising rather than on the current and future role of the institution. Yet the two are parts of the same whole—a healthy, effective organization. Intelligent campaign planning cannot ignore the availability of resources to support the objectives sought. Effective fundraising cannot take place if the organization cannot explain its intentions and how the gifts will be used to achieve them. Fundraising is a process, an assortment of methods, and a set of techniques, not an end in itself. Its success, and that of the organization it serves, depends on leading people of wealth, power, and influence to identify so strongly with achieving the purposes of the organization that they want to invest significant resources in it.

If an organization is to set useful, achievable, and challenging goals, it must know its purpose well and have a strong sense of what it must do to serve that purpose effectively in the future. Development staff should be essential to this process.

Organizational age and maturity

Newborn organizations often are only aware of those constituents who helped to get them started. Often the good people who establish not-for-profits do not have ties to people or organizations with wealth, power, and influence. Furthermore, new organizations are not well-known and established in the community, their purpose is not understood, and even among their own leadership there may be differences about direction and resources required.

A newborn must begin its goal setting by identifying and building a constituency. This can be done effectively during its initial planning and development efforts, but it cannot be ignored. The critical question, "Who's going to give this money?" cannot be left unanswered.

Mature organizations may suffer from inept goal setting as well. If, for instance, they have prospered for years by raising funds through the mail and special events, their potential for large-scale capital support may be limited. It will be difficult to convert loyal mail-responsive donors from the habit of writing checks for $25, $100, or even $1,000 into prospects for $25,000 or $100,000 or into donors of three- to five-year pledges. According to one school of thought, you renew and upgrade donors by the same method you used to acquire them. If this is the case—and we have seen some evidence that it is—then those contemplating a capital campaign will need to find ways to deal much more personally with their donors. And the conversion will take time—usually more than first anticipated.

Organizations supported by the proceeds of special events face an equally difficult situation. Buying a table, ticket, or journal ad appeals to a constituency that is often made up of people quite different from those who make large gift investments to support capital campaigns. The desire to be seen at the gala dinner-dance, entertain friends or clients at a social affair, or be visibly involved in honoring a high-powered community or corporate leader is not what motivates capital campaign support at the essential large-gift level.

All too often an organization supported in these ways gets the idea that a substantial endowment yielding good dividends and interest will take the pressure off it for annual mailings or events. It decides to launch an endowment campaign, frequently assuming that a substantial portion will come from planned gifts. Board members know how well their alma maters have done in attracting and building endowment; why not do the same for this social service agency? But with rare exceptions it isn't possible, and the exceptions are often rooted in a long-term program of promoting bequests to direct-mail donors. There is considerable anecdotal evidence that modest-level direct-mail donors leave surprisingly large bequests to organizations they only know through mail and the media.

Development program age and maturity

For a variety of reasons, established institutions sometimes lack strong development programs. They lose sight of or may be ignorant of the immaturity of their relationships with sources of support and expect that on the basis of prior service to the community they will be able to secure large sums as easily as other organizations that have built solid development relationships. Sometimes these organizations will have built their boards by assuring members that they will not have to raise funds or make gifts. In such cases, reshaping perceptions may have to come before fundraising. Although it is better to be favorably known than not known, relationships must be built, and this requires taking many of the same steps that newborn organizations must take and sometimes undoing some old perceptions. Changing institutional cultures is tough work! Nevertheless, all of this can be done.

The first step is to identify the obvious potential sources and construct a database. List systematically the board and staff members' friends; people and groups who benefit from the organization's mission; people, foundations, and corporations who take a civic interest and support a variety of programs for the good of the community; and community leaders whose records suggest a sympathy with the issues the institution seeks to address. Then find their "friends."

Every organization has a network of relationships, whether it knows it or not. The board and staff have card files and address books with the names of people they know, many of whom they have never thought of in the context of the organization they now wish to help. A close review of those names will turn up a number of people who would take time to listen to a presentation about the organization. (This is not to be a solicitation but rather an attempt to test ideas while planting seeds.) Then there are all the already well-known people in the community who can be asked to listen, especially if someone on the board or staff has a connection, or if one of the first layer of connections will use his or her "good offices" to open the door.

Organizations can graphically document the relationships discovered; this diagram can be set out as a network or spider web. Each connection reveals still more connections. As the title of the story goes, "six degrees of separation" or fewer are more than usually found between a worthy cause and people who, if they learn about it, will take an interest in it. (It should be noted that the purpose of identifying a constituency is not simply to assemble a huge list. The organization is looking for quality far more than quantity. Trying to find everybody who might support a cause is an especially misguided strategy at the outset of constituency building.)

Some counterintuitive advice applicable to all organizations

Although it is worthwhile to seek support from corporations and foundations, many organizations making their first foray into serious fundraising mistakenly assume that corporations and foundations will provide them with support far beyond the levels that other organizations have learned to expect from them. For most charitable organizations the principal sources of support are individuals and, unless there is an exceptionally good reason for thinking otherwise, that is where the organization should look first and most carefully.

Giving USA 1997 revealed that the $143 billion given in 1997 came from these sources:

Living individuals	$109 billion	76 percent
Bequests	$13 billion	9 percent
Foundations	$13 billion	9 percent
Corporations	$8 billion	6 percent

After accepting the implications of these data and becoming confident that a good list of prospective donors can be assembled, what must an organization do to build a base for capital campaigning and to begin to draw a bead on a goal?

Make a noise

Even the most altruistic people cannot respond if there is nothing to respond to or if they are completely ignorant about it. Announce the formation of the organization, the initiation of a strategic planning process, or an assessment of a condition the organization seeks to address. Get it in the media or send word of it to the "network" you've identified, using a letter from the person most effective in getting the message through to the intended recipient. Get word out that something special is going on in the organization or concerning the larger purpose it serves.

Send out a first cut of the plan or vision of the future

Send that plan, or better yet, *take it* to the people in the network, present it, and ask them to review it. Get back to them for comments. Keep developing drafts and circulating them to the network, expanding it as new connections are found. Listen to the comments that come back and accommodate as much as possible in the successive drafts. If a comment just won't "fly" in the organization, explain that it was considered and, if practical, tell why that choice wasn't made. To the greatest degree possible, let each successive draft reflect back to those commenting on it that their comments have been heard.

Some organizations worry that seeking the comments and observations of people who lack the expertise and cultural awareness of the organization's staff will subject it to pressure to do things that are unwise, disruptive, or in some cases, impossible. There have been highly publicized examples of this kind of pressure from time to time, but there are ways to avoid it or control it if that potential exists. One method is to start with a basic statement of the plan or vision that contains the essentials as the organization's leadership sees them. When discussing it with laypeople, know the difference between a different phrase and a different meaning.

Make it clear from the start that there are multiple voices to be heard, accommodations to be made to find workable solutions, and considerations in the field of endeavor within which the organization is to work. In all but the rarest of cases, this will be understood. In that rarest of cases where it is not and cannot be understood, end the relationship as gracefully as possible so that changes of personnel, heart, or understanding can lead to cooperation in the future. Last, of course, hold open the possibility that a person from "outside the box" might have a better idea.

By using this constituency identification process as a means of developing an institutional plan, the newborn organization or development program sets out and tests its case for support while assembling an informed and aware support group. It now has two of the most important prerequisites for setting goals effectively: a case and prospective donors who understand and appreciate the organization.

Institutional planning and sequence for implementation

Top-down analysis is often the first step management consultants take when examining the overall management of an institution rather than its fundraising specifically. This method assesses the development history, growth rates, or evidence of plateauing support, and projects that over five years a development program can raise two to three times the total raised in the previous five years in an aggressively conducted capital campaign. This rule-of-thumb technique, applied with an intelligent appreciation of the development history, can be a starting point or a ballpark estimate that gives some initial dimension to planning. However, if the goal-setting process stops here, without confirmation or elucidation by closer examination of the situation, the institution is at high risk of undertaking a half-baked campaign.

Gift range tables

Vilfredo Pareto (1848–1923), economist and sociologist, first promulgated what is today accepted as the 80/20 rule. That is, 20 percent of the effort produces 80 percent of the results. Sales managers usually agree: 20 percent of customers buy 80 percent of products; 20 percent of the sales force produces 80 percent of sales.

An article about New York's famed Bergdorf Goodman department store (Harris, 1985) cited these statistics: "There are some twenty customers who spend over six figures per year and another thirty who regularly spend over $50,000. The top 3 percent of Bergdorf customers account for 30 percent of the store's total sales, which are likely to exceed $100 million this year."

In a *New York Times* article ("Educated Consumers," 1995, p. D5) about banks and their profitability, the 80/20 rule was cited in these surprising terms: "Banc One, in Columbus, Ohio, found that its top 20 percent of customers provided 140 percent of its profits—and the remaining 80 percent cost it money."

Harold J. "Sy" Seymour (1894–1968), pioneering fundraising executive and consultant, developed the Rule of Thirds. In a memorandum written sometime around 1955, he noted, "As a rule of thumb, indicating the necessity for proportionate giving, about one-third of any capital [campaign] goal should be sought from the top ten to fifteen gifts, the next third from the next hundred gifts, and the last third from all other gifts."

In the 1960s, Princeton and Harvard conducted capital campaigns for what at the time were thought to be extraordinary goals.

The final results of each demonstrated the accuracy of Pareto's and Seymour's observations. For example:

- In Princeton's campaign (goal: $53,000,000) 27.0 percent of the goal was given by the top 10 donors, 39.0 percent was given by the next 100, and all others gave 33.0 percent. Furthermore, 21.3 percent of the 17,925 donors gave 96 percent of the $60.7 million raised (Seymour, 1988, p. 51).
- At Harvard (goal: $82,500,000) the top ten gave 28 percent, the next hundred gave 38 percent, and all others gave 34 percent (Seymour, 1988, p. 51).

Princeton's published report (McCleery, 1987) of its 1981 to 1986 campaign did not contain directly comparable data. However, it did note that of the total $330,000,000 raised, $177,314,000 was given by living individuals. The top twelve such gifts totaled $54,861,000 or 31.9 percent. Forty-two living individuals representing less than 1 percent of the 5,328 donors gave gifts of $1,000,000 or more, totaling $96,585,000 and amounting to 54 percent of the $177,314,000. Finally, 701 gifts of $25,000 or more accounted for just over $170,000,000. Thus, 13.2 percent of the 5,328 donors gave 96 percent of the funds received in this category.

The University of Richmond's published report cited these results for its 1989 to 1993 "Unfolding the Promise" campaign ("Unfolding the Promise," 1994). (See Table 4.1.)

Two tables from Kent Dove's book *Conducting a Successful Capital Campaign* (1988) depict the importance of top-level gifts even in one case when a single lead gift was not received. (See Tables 4.2 and 4.3.)

Current experience reveals a shift toward an ever-smaller percentage of donors providing an ever-larger percentage of the final results. In one recent typical example, a community hospital in Connecticut received $10,200,000 in 573 gifts and pledges; the twelve largest gifts from 2.1 percent of the donors accounted for $7,400,000 or 72.6 percent of the goal (Chris Collier, president,

Table 4.1. Results of the "Unfolding the Promise" campaign

Range of Gift	Number of Givers Goal	Number of Givers Actual	Amount
$20,000,000 and up	1	2	$67,336,200
$10,000,000–$19,999,999	2	1	$19,638,998
$5,000,000–$9,999,999	3	1	$6,612,500
$2,000,000–$4,999,999	4	3	$8,311,430
			Total: $101,899,128
$1,000,000–$1,999,999	10	12	$15,948,506
$750,000–$999,999	20	3	$2,425,140
$500,000–$749,999	30	15	$8,901,625
$250,000–$499,999	42	31	$10,012,205
			Total: $37,287,476
$100,000–$249,999	75	59	$7,740,692
$50,000–$99,999	200	68	$4,380,649
$25,000–$49,999	400	93	$3,081,789
$10,000–$24,999	700	205	$2,778,195
Under $10,000 More than 1,000		20,426	$7,443,557
			Total: $25,424,873
			Grand total: $164,611,477

Note: The top seven donors provided 61.9 percent of the total raised.

Table 4.2. Major gifts of a campaign with a goal of $51 million

Gift Range	Number of Gifts Required	Number of Gifts Received	Amount Required	Amount Received	Percentage of Goal
$1,000,000	10	12	$14,000,000	$19,200,000	35
$500,000	12	14	$7,000,000	$9,000,000	16
$100,000	80	82	$10,500,000	$15,100,000	28
$50,000	75	64	$5,000,000	$4,100,000	7
			$36,500,000	$47,400,000	86

Norwalk Hospital Foundation, Connecticut, personal communication with Robert Pierpont, June 1997).

So what does all this information about 80/20 and the Rule of Thirds have to do with goal setting today? It is perhaps as near as we can get to science in the art of fundraising, because it leads to the "test" of feasibility. Does your institution have sufficient prospects capable of giving the gifts needed to meet your goal? Does it have them now? Or can they be developed? If so, how and by when? The test procedure is to use a pro forma gift range table constructed to reflect the current pattern of successful campaigns:

Lead gifts   40 percent to 60 percent of goal
One lead gift   10 percent to 20 percent of goal
Two to three gifts   5 percent to 10 percent each
Four to six gifts   2.5 percent to 5 percent each
Midrange gifts   30 percent to 40 percent of goal
Thirty to sixty gifts   In three giving categories
Low-level gifts   10 percent to 20 percent of goal

A $1 million goal for a campaign with a three-year pledge period might start with a chart like the one shown in Table 4.4.

The test is to find out if you have prospective donors who could, if they would, give these gifts. A central question is this: How many prospective donors must you have for each gift to be confident that your goal is feasible?

In the past, a general rule was four to five prospects for each of the lead gifts, three to four for each of the midrange gifts, and two to three for the low-level gifts. The decreasing number needed as you moved down the chart was predicated on the idea that one of five prospects would give at the rated level and two or three would give at lower levels, therefore requiring fewer prospects for those levels.

Today, many institutions have such depth of experience with and knowledge of their prospects that they can be confident that each

Table 4.3. A campaign that succeeded without its lead major gift

	Gift Range	Donors Needed	Donors Committed	Total Gifts Requested	Total Gifts Received
Major gifts	$2,500,000	1	0	$2,500,000	—
	1,000,000	4	7	$4,000,000	$9,536,107
	500,000	4	4	$2,000,000	$2,500,000
	250,000	6	6	$1,500,000	$1,513,000
	150,000	10	10	$1,500,000	$1,934,520
Special gifts	100,000	23	12	$2,300,000	$1,319,890
	50,000	42	15	$2,100,000	$897,783
	25,000	54	35	$1,350,000	$1,031,990
	10,000	135	58	$1,350,000	$709,192
		279	147	$18,600,000	$19,442,484

Note: Numbers have been rounded.

Table 4.4. Pro forma gift range chart for a $1 million campaign

Number of Gifts	Amount of Each Gift	Amount from Level	Cumulative Amount	Percent of Total
1	$150,000	$150,000	$150,000	
1	$75,000	$75,000	$225,000	
2	$60,000	$120,000	$345,000	
4	$30,000	$120,000	$465,000	46.5
8	$15,000	$120,000	$585,000	
16	$7,500	$120,000	$705,000	
32	$3,000	$96,000	$801,000	33.6
64	$1,500	$96,000	$897,000	
100	$600	$60,000	$957,000	
Many	Less than $600	$43,000	$1,000,000	19.9

top gift will be given by a single prospect. In many cases these gifts are being negotiated even as the campaign is being planned. At the lower levels, however, many more than three, four, or five prospects are needed because in campaigns with hundreds or thousands of prospective donors much less is known about the gift capacity of the mass of prospects. They are less involved and will be solicited impersonally by mail, phone, or both. Ten, twenty, or more prospects may be needed for gifts at the bottom of the chart.

Knowing well and involving deeply the prospects for the top ten to twenty gifts is necessary because they very well may be the key to goal setting. Why? Because setting the final goal can be a product of how much is given by these lead donors, individually and in aggregate.

Feasibility studies

The feasibility study is the classic step for many institutions to determine goals. It is normally conducted by a fundraising consulting firm retained by the institution to do an objective and confidential assessment of its capability to raise a large goal over a specified period of years, usually three to five and not more than seven. The institution and the study director from the firm develop together a list of those people close to the institution whose support—financial, volunteer, and moral—will be decisive to the success of a campaign.

A letter seeking an hour-long confidential interview with the consultant will be prepared to be signed by either a key volunteer or an executive of the organization. The firm and the consultant will develop lists of prospects (individual, corporate, and foundation) for significant gifts from each of these constituencies and a list of prospective volunteers to secure these gifts.

The consultant then prepares a gift range table showing what is needed at each level of the gift pyramid in order for the campaign to be successful. This will be shown to respondents to assist them in understanding the level of gifts they and others will be asked to make and to secure respondents' best estimates of the potential levels of support that might be provided by the listed prospective donors. If more than one goal is being considered, tables will be prepared for each. In some cases respondents will indicate the level of their anticipated support after looking at the table.

The institution prepares a brief draft of a case for support, that is, a brief statement of the larger purposes it expects to achieve as a result of a successful campaign and persuasive arguments for why these things should be done and be done now. This statement will have a tentative goal or goals for the respondents to consider. This draft will be sent to the interviewees for review in advance of their confidential interview with the consultant. Once the letters are sent, appointments are set by the organization and the interviews are conducted. The consultants prepare and deliver a report of their observations and recommendations.

At its most precise, the recommendation on the goal will set out a number and a time frame for its achievement. But not all feasibility studies, and especially those for newer organizations and programs, point clearly to a single number. Interviews with some of the highest-potential prospects for gifts may suggest important steps that the organization will need to take to secure optimal gifts; the goal revealed in the interviews may be inadequate to meet the organization's needs as set out in the case; the constituency may regard the case as too timid and be prepared to exceed the tested goal if the organization will act more boldly.

In these cases, the recommendation may be to set out several goals that might be publicized when the campaign is announced publicly if certain specified benchmark conditions have been met by certain dates during the quiet or advance-gifts phase of the campaign. Normally these conditions will require that certain levels of support be forthcoming early (by a specified date) from the board and the close family of the organization, that prospects for additional gifts be identified in the ratio of five-to-one or three-to-one for achieving either the next phase of the campaign or the full goal, and that some number of prospects be actively under cultivation. The recruitment of key leaders might be another specified condition. Obviously, in those instances where changes to the plan or case could alter the goal, those would be reflected in new drafts for consideration. Each of the specified dates is occasion for making a go or no-go decision about a higher-level goal at the time of public announcement.

Who's going to give the money?

Even when all the signs point to a specific goal number and time period, a question remains: Who is this money going to come from, specifically, and how do we make sure that our answer to this question can be relied upon?

The feasibility study, confirmed and added to by the observations of informed volunteers and staff, will have identified several key prospects for significant gifts. A specific strategy for seeking gifts from each of these people and organizations should be developed. A range of gift potential should be predicted for each and the total of these should be summed, thus providing a measure of the overall potential from this group.

The process that has proven effective in recent situations involves setting a goal by conducting a small-scale "experimental" campaign, testing and refining the case, and engaging, cultivating, and soliciting the highest-potential prospects. A goal based on the outcome of this effort can be substantially higher than originally imagined if high-level support received early in the process is contagious, inspiring leadership to press ahead with further solicitations. If these result in still greater success, the first established goal can be revisited and probably increased. The process works best when it is anticipated and planned with an initial level of support set as an interim goal to be celebrated when it is achieved and raised if high-level prospects remain uncommitted or unsolicited. A new goal is set and then, when it is achieved and if prospects remain, the bar can be raised even higher. This step-by-step approach to goal setting based on success with the small percentage of donors who will provide 80 percent to 90 percent or more of the overall goal is effective and cost-effective. No brochures are needed. The impact of the aggregate raised before the kickoff will evoke a *wow!* when the campaign is announced.

Ultimately, the moving target comes to rest when high-potential volunteer leaders and prospective donors have reached consensus on the case and the campaign's objectives, when the goal has been tested and proven feasible, when significant pace-setting lead gifts have been secured, and when volunteer committees for the public phase of the campaign have been organized.

References

Council for Advancement and Support of Education. *CASE Management Reporting Standards: Standards for Annual Giving and Campaigns in Education Fundraising.* Washington, D.C.: Council for Advancement and Support of Education, Feb. 1996.

Council for Advancement and Support of Education. *Fundraising Standards for Annual Giving and Campaign Reports for Not-for-Profit Organizations Other Than Colleges, Universities, and Schools.* Washington, D.C.: Council for Advancement and Support of Education, Apr. 1998.

Dove, K. E. *Conducting a Successful Capital Campaign.* San Francisco: Jossey-Bass, 1988.

"Educated Consumers." *The New York Times,* June 5, 1995, p. D5.

Giving USA 1997. New York: American Association of Fund-Raising Counsel Trust for Philanthropy, 1997.

Harris, L. "Bergdorf Goodman, the One and Only." *Town and Country,* Sept. 1985.

McCleery, W. *The Story of a Campaign for Princeton.* Princeton, N.J.: Princeton University Press, 1987.

Seymour, H. J. *Designs for Fund Rising* (2nd ed.). Rockville, Md.: Fundraising Institute, 1988.

"Unfolding the Promise." *The Campaign for the University of Richmond.* Richmond, Va.: University of Richmond Development Office, 1994.

ROBERT PIERPONT *is chairman and CEO of Pierpont & Wilkerson, Ltd., a fundraising consulting firm located outside New York City in Garrison, New York.*

G. STEVEN WILKERSON *is president of Pierpont & Wilkerson, Ltd.*

It is possible to avoid information overload in a major campaign and the mental paralysis that it can precipitate. An effective campaign information system organizes the necessary information and discounts the rest.

5

Information systems: Managing the database

Scott Lange, Charles Hunsaker

AN INFORMATION MANAGEMENT SYSTEM is essential for managing campaign information in today's computer age. In the first section of this chapter, Scott Lange discusses the characteristics of an effective information management system. In the second section, Charles Hunsaker discusses the hardware and software options available to a development professional.

Campaign information in the computer age

When I started my first campaign as director of development for Roanoke College, the vice president sent over copies of his correspondence to potential donors with a handwritten note on each that read, "Put this person into the system." Not knowing what that system was, where it was located, or how someone would get "into it," I put the letters into file folders. This was our first system.

NEW DIRECTIONS FOR PHILANTHROPIC FUNDRAISING, NO. 21, FALL 1998 © JOSSEY-BASS PUBLISHERS

As we started soliciting more people, the number of file folders grew and the need for a more sophisticated process became apparent. If we were to be organized, make prospect assignments, set priorities, design solicitation plans, track progress, and avoid chaos, a true system was essential. Though it was easy to become distracted by other activities, without a system, interaction with prospects would be sporadic and ill-planned. So I designed a "prospect information system" to organize our efforts and follow the sequential process of major gift fundraising.

I began by accepting the maldistribution principle of campaign fundraising—that 80 percent of gifts would come from 20 percent of donors. In fact, when I examined our donor base, I discovered that 90 percent of our gift revenue was being contributed by less than 1.5 percent of our donors. In our case, this meant that thirty-five families (out of an alumni population of thirty thousand) were contributing most of the money. As a consequence, I designed the initial campaign management system to track the top 1.5 percent of our donors—those who had already demonstrated their commitment to the college by virtue of their giving.

We knew from our gift range chart that we needed a total of 250 donors to complete our campaign. We also knew that we would need an average of 4 prospects for every donor. In other words, when asking for a gift we could expect 1 out of 4 prospects to give the requested amount. We multiplied the number of gifts required by four and discovered that we would need 1,000 prospects to complete the campaign. Our initial donor list of 35 thus had to be expanded to 1,000 prospects. The design of our prospect management system had to include the top 35 prospects plus another 965 prospects selected from our thirty-thousand-person constituent pool. To avoid information overload, we developed a system that included only the portion of the constituency deemed most likely to make a campaign gift. The system worked, and our campaign succeeded.

At that time, which was early in the computer revolution, the discoveries we made as we designed our prospect information system seemed innovative and even extraordinary. Today, the ideas behind the system serve as the basis for commercial computer software programs designed specifically to support capital campaigns.

Philanthropy: An emotional process

Philanthropy is the tangible evidence of an emotional event. The root derivations, the Greek words *philos* and *anthropos*, combine to mean *love of humanity*. Development is the business of discovering those things that are important to the constituents of an organization and showing them how they can work with that organization to improve the human condition. An effective campaign management system, therefore, is much more than lists of prospects and meetings. An effective campaign management system is devoted to the process of discerning a prospect's rationale for giving and creating an environment that will inspire the prospect to make substantial charitable investments.

Prospect management systems for large campaigns begin by helping to identify and filter those people whom the campaign officers, chief executive, and board members should get to know. They capture information, help plan and manage prospect activity, support volunteer activity, and develop reports about campaign progress.

Prospect information: Combining art and science

The prospect management system must facilitate the collection, synthesis, and presentation of data to the people who will need it to cultivate or solicit a prospect. Campaign information systems help bring science to the art of cultivating relationships between prospects and an organization. A prospect information system collects both basic biographical information about the prospect and information about why the prospect might be willing and motivated to invest in the organization.

Basic data about prospects include answers to the following questions: What are their full names and titles? Where do they live? Where do they work? To whom are they related? Names, addresses, phone numbers, occupations, employers, and birth dates are all essential information. These data can also include information on the prospects' estimated income and assets; where they went to school; their age; and their children, including their number, names, and ages. Some development offices may wish to gather information about the prospect's parents, and whether the prospect has taken on a financial commitment to care for them in retirement, hospital care, or nursing care.

More in-depth information about prospects, their lives, belief systems, and preferences, is also vital in developing an effective prospect plan. This might include all or some of the following:

- What they believe is important
- How they are involved with the organization
- The people they respect at the organization
- Whether they believe in the mission and vision of the organization
- Their giving patterns
- Their religious beliefs
- Their social contacts
- Their professional and recreational interests

Much of this information is gathered through personal meetings with prospects and then supplemented by basic research techniques, market research, electronic screenings, peer-review screenings, focus groups, or attitude surveys. The result of the discovery process is recorded in a research profile that helps the development staff make informed decisions about how and when to ask for philanthropic support.

Prospect management: The pipeline concept

Prospect management is the process of encouraging and monitoring the progress of prospects through the stages of the solicitation cycle. The solicitation cycle is the progression of steps or stages through which prospects move. With some allowances for a personal preference in nomenclature, the steps include these: identification, research, strategic planning, cultivation, solicitation, acknowledgment, stewardship, and renewal.

At Cornell University, David Dunlop refined the process of monitoring the progress of prospective donors through the solicitation cycle and dubbed it *moves management*. The essence of a moves management system is the concept of tracking the "moves" that a prospect makes through the solicitation cycle. A move occurs when a prospect's status changes. For example a prospect might move from "Cultivate" to "Ready to Solicit" to "Proposal Pending" to "Acknowledgment" to "Stewardship" as they progress through the solicitation cycle.

An effective prospect information system provides a simple, effective way to track this progress. At any professional conference on campaign fundraising, the presenter will report that it takes seven or eight personal visits to secure a major campaign commitment. A prospect management system, therefore, must be able to record a series of meetings with each prospect over the course of a three- or five-year campaign. Each meeting must be scheduled and planned, and the observations and results from each must be recorded.

An effective prospect management system will categorize prospective donors according to where they are in the solicitation cycle. Many development operations find themselves in a situation where they have a few major donors (mostly trustees) who are ready to be solicited. The trustees are a known and easy group to place in the solicitation cycle. But because less is known about other good prospects, they are more difficult to categorize. The balance of the constituency is at the other end of the continuum—that is, unknown. After identifying the top tiers of prospects, the prospect management system helps to spread these prospective donors throughout the solicitation cycle. Some prospects may be placed directly into the "Cultivate" stage, others are "Ready to Solicit," and many fall under the "Research" or "Strategic Planning" categories. Under optimal conditions, organizations will have prospects at every stage of the solicitation cycle. New prospects are continually introduced into the pipeline. Existing prospects are moved to the next level of engagement, and occasionally some prospects are removed.

Having prospects at each stage of the cycle throughout the pipeline permits a steady stream of solicitations during a campaign. An effective system brings focus and discipline to this process.

Strategic planning: Prospect by prospect

A campaign information system also provides a mechanism for two types of planning. First, it enables the campaign office to assign prospects to staff and volunteer solicitors and to track their activity and progress. Second, it provides a means to plan action steps to move the prospects through the solicitation cycle.

Staff assignments are often based on the information in the prospect's research profile and the development officer's caseload. Some organizations split account responsibility by geographic region, others by the prospects' area of interest in the institution, others still by the personal interaction between the prospect and staff member.

Whatever methods are used to assign prospects to staff and volunteers to prospects, they must provide for three roles: account manager, coach, and solicitor. The account manager is responsible for the creation and execution of the strategic plan for the prospect. This role falls to a development officer. The coach provides insight on the prospect and suggestions on how to approach and work with the prospect, as well as a candid assessment of the job done. Usually, this job falls to a volunteer. Finally, someone must ask for the gift. Many experts argue that the most effective solicitors are volunteers who solicit their peers. Increasingly, however, staff members and chief executive officers are soliciting gifts. A complete information system will track each of these roles and provide a planned approach to prospect management.

A sound prospect plan will also include a cultivation strategy, anticipated outcomes, and a solicitation strategy. The solicitation plan determines what the prospect should be asked for in terms of amount, purpose, and recognition; who should make the request; and when the request should be made.

The plan must be available to all those working with the prospect: development officers to help design solicitation strategies, plan meetings, and schedule next steps, and volunteers for the information they need for prospect meetings.

Reporting: Record of the past, guide to the future

A good campaign management system must include a contact log to provide the chronology of every meeting, correspondence, and interaction with each prospect. The contact log simplifies the reporting process and provides an excellent basis for reviewing prospect progress at staff meetings. A tickler or calendar system keeps track of upcoming contacts and provides information that keeps prospects from falling between the cracks.

Finally, a campaign management system has to track campaign progress. An effective system provides easy and accurate information about how many solicitations have been made, resulting pledges, solicitations in progress, and anticipated outcomes. Configuring this information into a gift range chart, the system provides valuable information about the progress, activity, and potential of the campaign.

Some prospect management systems also handle gift processing, accounting, acknowledgment, and pledge reminders. In other systems, these functions are part of a more comprehensive development and accounting system. In either case, these functions are critical to the success of a campaign. They must be handled accurately and with ample opportunity to personalize correspondence.

Selecting the right system

The first section of this chapter talked about the types of campaign elements that an information system should support. These included (1) capturing and maintaining background information from either research or electronic screening; (2) maintaining contact reminders and call reports; (3) supporting volunteer management; and (4) assisting with campaign reporting. What options does an institution have to deliver these capabilities to its users?

System options

Organizations have three main options when they select a system: *homegrown systems, comprehensive systems,* and *off-the-shelf modules.*

Option 1: Homegrown, do-it-yourself. Smaller grassroots organizations may cobble together a system from one of the PC-based suites of products that include a word processor, spreadsheet, database, and calendar or personal information manager (PIM). The word processor may be used for all kinds of letters and contact reports, the database or spreadsheet may be used to maintain key information on donors and prospects, and the PIM may help remind development officers of upcoming events and things to do. This can work; even the largest development shops will use some of these tools. However, this is like saying that a pencil with an eraser is the ultimate word processor; it will work but it gets quite cumbersome as the volumes of work increase. Further, these cobbled-together solutions don't handle very well—or at all—gift and pledge processing, campaign reporting, or any of the more complex campaign requirements.

Option 2: Comprehensive systems. At the other end of the scale, many larger institutions use a comprehensive development database system. This may support alumni and development operations for colleges and universities, membership and development operations in membership organizations, or just development in others. These complete systems range from simple single-user PC-based applications, to more comprehensive client-server applications, to minicomputer or mainframe applications.

The comprehensive development systems that support campaign operations have complete gift-processing modules to deal with everything from routine gift and pledge processing up to the most complex transactions involving deferred gifts, multiyear commitments, and gift splits to multiple designations (for example, with endowment, capital, and annual fund components). They handle the legal or "hard" credits that the IRS and their accounting departments track as well as the recognition or "soft" credits recognizing multiple donors for the same gift.

Some of the systems even summarize or aggregate giving on a nightly basis in various categories, such as campaign, campaign by year, fund within campaign, appeal within campaign, source or constituent type within campaign, and so on. This type of summation provides the foundation for a *data warehouse*, which facilitates comprehensive analyses in a very complex campaign environment. A data warehouse should provide access to consistent data, gathered over time, with tools to query, analyze, and present information. It should allow users to "slice and dice" data in any way desired (Kimball, 1996, p. xxvi.) In institutions with hundreds of thousands of donors and prospects, and perhaps millions of financial transactions, this type of approach is nearly imperative to provide the timely analysis and reporting needed for a significant campaign.

Most comprehensive development system vendors have organized screens or tables to capture and maintain research and screening information in their systems. Different systems have different ways to capture free-text or noncoded data into their systems. Some merely have a general "notepad" where users can record anything and must establish procedural guidelines for formatting their notes. Others have specific places in their systems for financial notes, family notes, and notes from call reports.

The comprehensive development systems may integrate accounting, membership, student, human resource, or other systems with the development application. This allows gift information to flow to the accounting system accurately in accordance with Financial Accounting Standards Board guidelines. Staff pledges can automatically translate to payroll deductions. Student systems, membership systems, or ticketing systems can also automatically input their constituents into the development system.

Institutions can build interfaces to their other applications, but a single vendor should be able to deliver the cleanest and most tightly coupled interfaces. Most stand-alone development packages have tools or modules to facilitate certain of these interfaces. The debate over "best-of-breed versus integrated systems" is outside the scope of this chapter. There are benefits to both solutions and the right choice depends on the institution's requirements.

Many systems today also facilitate contact tracking, moves management, or prospect management. In a comprehensive development system, when contact tracking is entered once everyone has immediate access to the same prospect data. This built-in function gives prospect managers complete access to the most up-to-date giving information, relationships, calls or visits by other development personnel, proposals, or plans for cultivation initiatives.

A number of major fundraising consulting firms, though, offer or recommend stand-alone prospect management systems. They argue that a simpler database of your top X hundred prospects doesn't need to contain all of the information of the comprehensive system. It just needs to provide the key information for planning, cultivating, and moving these individuals from prospect to donor to major donor. Maybe this is why we all carry laptop computers and not desktops on the road.

Option 3: Off-the-shelf modules. Stand-alone contact management systems are widely used for sales management (for example, ACT!, Goldmine, and others) as well for fundraising. Some institutions use the database tools noted in Option 1 to build their own simple systems.

There are a number of benefits to off-the-shelf modules. They are usually simpler to use than the prospect management modules of comprehensive development systems. Both generic sales management and fundraising-specific prospect management systems contain basic name, address, and other biographical information about the prospects. They have the means to enter ticklers or reminders of calls, meetings, and other things to do. They are able to record a contact or call report and the next step after a contact is made. In the sales management systems, user-definable fields record such data as interests, wealth indicators, and limited giving history. Prospect management systems have these fields already defined.

For the traveling development officer with a laptop, these systems support remote use with later synchronization to a master database. This means that development officers can use their system while on the road or in a plane without connecting to a host system. They can focus on fundraising with less worry about modems, Internet connections, and the like. But as mentioned earlier, these systems may not have the most complete or up-to-date information and they usually maintain limited gift information. Users must decide which features are more important to them.

Hardware and software

Clients often ask system consultants for advice in selecting the right hardware and software for their systems. Their query reflects a growing level of sophistication. Just five years ago, consultants were most often asked to recommend software to go along with the hardware the clients had already acquired. Today, most organizations are taking the more effective approach and selecting the hardware required to run their chosen development application and general-purpose (office automation) software.

To select development software, users and technical staff must work together to define their functional and performance requirements. They must solicit vendor bids through either a request for information or a request for proposal (often merely called RFI or RFP), and they must evaluate the vendors and their systems by reviewing their proposals, viewing demonstrations, and calling or visiting other users (Pressman, 1992, p. 117).

In selecting general-purpose software, it is most important to standardize systems within an office. It doesn't matter if WordPerfect or Word is selected as the word processor, or if Freelance Graphics or Powerpoint is the presentation tool. But it does matter that everyone agrees to use the same version of the same tool! Standardization allows people to share data without gnashing teeth and yelling because their file gets reformatted or cannot be read at all. It minimizes the need for training and facilitates the sharing of knowledge and experience as well as data.

In addition to the general-purpose software, standardization helps in other systems areas as well. System users have benefitted from the standardization of Windows, which most vendors and users now have on their desktops. Along with the Windows operating system running on these machines, Microsoft has provided low-cost copies of MS-Office to many schools and other nonprofits. Many of the vendors of larger and comprehensive development systems have also standardized on Oracle or SQL Server as their underlying database management system. This facilitates sharing information throughout an organization and reduces support required for multiple databases.

Hardware purchases should be based on the requirements of the software that has been selected. Regardless of the type of system (PCs, servers, or minicomputers), value is measured by memory size, processor speed, and disk space. Hardware should be purchased that provides more memory and speed than the "minimum required."

Development officers who spend a great deal of time on the road often have special computing needs. Whether the institution has selected a comprehensive system that these road warriors must connect to or a stand-alone system for prospect management, the traveling development officer may want to access e-mail or otherwise contact home base from the road. This requires a modem connection of at least 28.8 kbs in speed and an extra length of phone cord and connectors for inconveniently placed phones in hotel rooms or connections to phones in frequent-flier lounges. A "techie" from the development services office or the institution's information services department can set up the right dialing and connection software on the laptop. Rather than carrying a portable printer, many laptop users install fax software and fax their documents to themselves at the hotel where they are staying to provide a quick hard copy of their work.

A techie will also be able to set up the software on the receiving end. A number of development offices are using and suggesting a product called Citrix Winframe, which allows users to dial into a host computer remotely and run applications just as if they were on their laptops. Other vendors recommend browser-based systems (for example, Netscape or Internet Explorer) to allow inquiry, reporting, and even updating the development database via the Internet or an intranet. Of course, Internet access requires special security and additional administrative support for use.

Training

Information systems are like a three-legged stool. Many people think of hardware and software as "the system," but they represent only one leg of the stool. The second leg is infrastructure—management commitment, resource budget, and policies and procedures. The third leg is the users—the trained, competent, available users. As is characteristic of a three-legged stool, all of the legs must be of the same length or the stool will not be in balance and may topple over. Only with all the legs in balance can you have a reliable system with accurate data.

In this analogy, which rings true for many people, training is very important. Though it is not necessary to train everyone in all aspects of the system, all users must have the right training to use most effectively the systems that pertain to their work. The best hardware and software is worth little if the users do not know how to use it.

The importance of training on the productivity and effectiveness of computer systems cannot be emphasized enough. Strassmann in *The Squandered Computer* notes that expenditures for technology have *no* correlation with either profitability or productivity! However, he calculates that of the over $1 trillion spent on information technology worldwide in 1996, only 2 percent was spent on training (Strassmann, 1997, p. 26). We believe this is a key factor in Strassmann's conclusions.

Similarly, Wang notes that much of the disconnect between MIS and users comes from the fact that users don't know how to use the tools that are being provided (Wang, 1994, p. xviii). Users must have a base level or set of core competencies in the technologies they are using. They must be provided with and take advantage of training on both the campaign system and the general-office systems to make full and effective use of all the systems.

Staffing

Adequate, technically trained staff must be available to deliver and support the technologies. Staffing must be determined by the work to be done and balanced against the time frames desired for completion. Advancement vice presidents make these decisions routinely for fundraising. Unfortunately, all too often the responsibilities for systems are merely assigned to the existing staff.

Though the cost of individual machines is plummeting, the total cost of computing may be increasing. The real five-year cost of computing may be $20,000 or more. Of this, only $2,000 to $6,000 shows up as the cost of acquisition, supplies, and in-house technical assistance. Studies note that peer support may cost two to three times this amount, or $6,000 to $15,000. If there is not a specific support person, users turn to the so-called guru or super users in their offices for support. This practice often "steals" hours of productive development time, redirecting it to reactive technical assistance. In networking environments the support demand is multiplied, as is the stolen time factor, if a specialist is not designated to handle the technical and training functions (Tenner, 1996, p. 198).

As development offices look to add the kind of technology required to manage large campaigns today, they must include technology support staff in their planning. With more and more dependence on technology, support staff must be available to train users; maintain the hardware, software, and data; and assist responsively when things go wrong.

Conclusion

Computers and well-managed databases enable staff and volunteers to be more effective by gathering and organizing information quickly, reducing paperwork, making sources of relevant information easily accessible, and structuring cultivation and solicitation plans. Put to proper use, the increased efficiency and information will enable the development professional to do a better job of building the relationships that are at the heart of their work. Computers and systems are great tools, but development is about people. Woe to those who subordinate the inherent personal, emotional, and human nature of this work to information management systems!

References

Kimball, R. *The Data Warehouse Toolkit.* New York: Wiley, 1996.

Pressman, R. S. *Software Engineering: A Practitioner's Approach.* New York: McGraw-Hill, 1992.

Strassmann, P. A. (ed.). *The Squandered Computer.* New Canaan, Conn.: Information Economics Press, 1997.

Tenner, E. *Why Things Bite Back: Technology and the Revenge of Unintended Consequences.* New York: Knopf, 1996.

Wang, C. *Techno Vision: The Executive's Survival Guide to Understanding and Managing Information Technology.* New York: McGraw-Hill, 1994.

SCOTT LANGE *is a former major gifts officer and now president of Institutional Memory, a software firm offering Gifted Memory, a system for prospect tracking and management.*

CHARLES HUNSAKER *is president of R. I. Arlington, a consulting firm providing systems consulting to development offices and nonprofit organizations.*

Although small and grassroots organizations often face serious development challenges, combining their special strengths with traditional techniques can carry them through a successful campaign.

6

Working from strength: How small organizations succeed with big campaigns

Christine P. Graham

TO READ THE NONPROFIT NEWSLETTERS and magazines today one would think the sector is primarily populated with large-scale national nonprofits, aggressive fundraising colleges, and universities and medical centers. The fact is, one pure piece of Americana is our propensity for establishing small, community-based organizations to serve our very local needs.

Vermont, where I do most of my work, is an extreme illustration of this behavior. In a recent study, INDEPENDENT SECTOR and the Urban Institute found that Vermont has the highest density of nonprofits per capita nationally: fifteen organizations per 10,000 population. Doing the math, then, shows that this state of approximately 600,000 residents would have nine hundred nonprofits. Although this may sound impressive, the study actually underestimated the total. According to our secretary of state records, there are over five thousand nonprofits established, or one for every 120 residents.

NEW DIRECTIONS FOR PHILANTHROPIC FUNDRAISING, NO. 21, FALL 1998 © JOSSEY-BASS PUBLISHERS

Vermont's rurality and geographic challenges to easy travel combined with the well-known crusty independence of New Englanders yield a tendency to start more small nonprofits rather than a few larger ones. But although the trend is more extreme here, it is not idiosyncratic. Whereas buyouts, mergers, and near-monopolies sweep the country in the commercial realm, in the nonprofit sector local organizations continue to struggle to thrive, knowing there is a special spirit to a community-based effort.

These small organizations are admirable, but they face daunting financial challenges. Perhaps most threatening is their need for major capital expansion in building, endowment, and programmatic growth. When those needs become undeniable, small, young, and community-based nonprofits turn to capital campaigns: big campaigns that may dwarf their previous fundraising experiences.

In Vermont, a state with the highest per-capita level of nonprofits—a state ranked the most rural among all states—where the majority have been established since the early 1970s, capital campaigns are a relatively new phenomenon. Most of the organizations I encounter have never undertaken a capital campaign before. Most do not have aggressive annual drives, and nearly all are understaffed, work with old-fashioned systems, and are unaccustomed to sophisticated development techniques, including prospect research or economic impact studies. Yet they are highly successful in meeting community needs. Our market is full of the small, young, and grassroots organizations that I refer to as "novice" campaigners in this chapter.

Capital campaigns conducted by grassroots organizations and other small, young, community-based nonprofits can be both scary and powerfully rewarding. At first glance, we have to believe that the odds are against success because these undercapitalized and often understaffed novice groups have so few of the technical strengths professionals like to see in a precampaign audit. But with the right encouragement and direction the accomplishments can be astounding, because these nonmainstream groups have other assets that compensate for the technical challenges.

A strong, professional approach to fundraising values both the art *and* the science of development, moving gracefully between the two approaches. Most organizations rely more heavily on one or the other. Often an established and experienced organization relies on the "science" of fundraising, capitalizing on its depth of professional staffing, sophisticated recording systems, research capacity, and carefully rated donor and prospect lists. If anything, the organization may need to revive the passion of staff and volunteers.

Start-up groups weigh in more heavily on the "art" side of the equation. Software, giving records, experienced volunteers, and rated prospect lists are foreign concepts to these groups, but the spirit, devotion, passion . . . there's the strength! This deep level of commitment can take an organization a very long way.

But during an intense, major fundraising campaign, their fundraising deficiencies often present serious challenges. These novice organizations must emphasize and capitalize on their passion while building the technical side of the fundraising program. In the process, the organization evolves to a new level of professionalism.

In preparation for writing this chapter, I surveyed fifteen of my colleagues in Vermont, where nonprofits by definition are non-mainstream. In this chapter, I rely heavily on their responses to my survey and on my own experiences. Not an entirely scientific method, perhaps, but one that is in keeping with the nonscientific approach typical of our organizations.

Organizations outside the mainstream

There are a variety of nontraditional candidates for capital campaigns, and the wise professional will identify and analyze their characteristics before planning one. The challenge is to find ways to adapt and bend traditional campaign practices so the identity of the organization is not lost, while the goal is met and the development operation is strengthened for the long haul.

Though young grassroots organizations share many characteristics, they also have important differences that can present particular roadblocks and challenges to campaign planning. These organizations fall into three categories: the *perennially small*, the *true grassroots*, and the *start-up*.

Perennially small organizations

Perennially small organizations have only limited ability to expand. The limitations on growth might come from the comfort and safety in keeping an organization small. Or they may come from very real geographic and demographic limitations—rurality, for example.

In some organizations, key board members have a vested interest in not letting the organization outgrow them. They often think it is possible to stay small while becoming highly sophisticated and financially stable. As long as they can reach their short-term goals, their expectations remain modest and they have a high level of satisfaction with the organization.

These organizations often do not communicate their message far beyond their members, donors, and beneficiaries. These small organizations are often challenged to find an adequate donor base for a stretch campaign.

True grassroots organizations

A true grassroots organization need not be small. Most essential to its nature is an egalitarian membership that drives the mission and activities of the organization. It is characterized by a bottom-heavy gift chart in annual giving, with a disproportionately small number of major donors. In fact, most grassroots organizations are committed to the belief that many members giving at lower levels should be able to support their work, contrary to traditional fundraising theory and practice. As a result, much of the fundraising is conducted on a less personal level, and cultivation of major donors is rare. However, a vast number of members know intimately the workings of the organization and feel deeply committed to it.

Start-up nonprofits

New nonprofits often look like the grassroots organizations, but after a short time most grow and develop the governance and operating structure of a more traditional or mainstream institution. This evolution is often precipitated by a capital campaign. The egalitarian base of support characteristic of a grassroots organization is excellent for a start-up but often does not lead to accomplishing the organization's mission. Therefore, in the early years, many organizations begin to build up their giving pyramid by cultivating and soliciting midlevel and major gifts. They thus begin to outgrow the grassroots phase and are happy to do so. Embarking on a capital campaign midway through this transition is a challenge, but it is not culturally difficult for the board and the members of the group.

All three types of organizations face challenges when they undertake capital campaigns. The greatest of these challenges are common to all of them: a lack of experience in raising major gifts and the need for the type of leadership that facilitates top solicitations. The defining characteristics of these organizations serve to amplify these two issues, creating a lot of organizational anxiety.

Whatever their differences, one day it becomes clear that the organization cannot continue to serve its constituents without attracting or creating a major asset: a building, an endowment, a scholarship fund, or another capital venture.

In most small and grassroots organizations the need grows over a long period of time, because the organization is not oriented toward capital enhancement or major fundraising. The board may be afraid of the work or feel it would destroy the organization's image. The board members cannot see the investment value of hiring professional counsel, and the fees horrify them. Often, they'll try to raise capital gifts on their own but are limited by inexperience and a lack of effective fundraising knowledge and systems. The need continues to increase, and operations are severely hampered. Eventually they grasp at the possibility of a campaign as a saving grace.

Fundraising characteristics at the onset of planning

Because all internal forces of the organization have resisted a capital campaign for some time, by the time the board finally faces the reality of conducting a campaign, the organization's needs have become critical. In these organizations, the idea of a major campaign seldom evolves gradually from a long-range strategic planning process but rather stems from urgent need. They have become accustomed to fueling much of their work with devotion, sacrifice, and their passion and courage. Therefore, the fundraising readiness of grassroots organizations tends to lag far behind the "readiness" of their need.

Usually, these organizations have small and reliable but shallow donor pools with little or no history of major-gift fundraising. These organizations often fear fundraising and have a real aversion to soliciting gifts face-to-face and to asking for specific amounts. Annual goals inch up over the years but are seldom designed to improve the fiscal health of the organization dramatically. Grassroots organizations are particularly reluctant to appear too well-funded or too aggressive.

Much of this behavior springs from patterns established by the board. The board members of these organizations often were— or are—deeply involved in implementing the program, were founders of the group, and give "time instead of money." Although many board members may not have great wealth, others may be giving very generously elsewhere and do not want to stand out in the nondonor culture. A capital campaign provides an excellent opportunity to change the culture of board giving, providing a clear and shared opportunity for board members to make major financial contributions in addition to contributing their time and hard work.

Although many small organizations can make up for a nongiving board culture through training and education as they prepare for a campaign, true grassroots organizations, wedded in principle to broad-base funding, face a bigger challenge. For these organizations, the price of major-gift fundraising may be too high philosophically. As noted earlier, they often wish to remain supported at a lower level by many members and by grants rather than risk the power shift that sometimes comes with major gifts. Capital campaigns are not egalitarian operations, and landmark goals cannot be met without a few major gifts in addition to healthy giving at all levels of the pyramid.

Only a terrifically strong need and compelling case will convince the board to veer from its traditions. This powerful case is often underlined by a sense of desperation, and the possibility of losing the entire organization, which adds a frantic nature to the campaign but certainly can help create leadership.

Traps and threats

In addition to a sense of urgency, desperation, or overconfidence, other dangerous patterns are common to organizations that are novices when it comes to campaigning. The leadership and consultants are wise to take these traps seriously, for in small organizations a magnifying glass is suspended over each problem: what might simply disappear in a capital campaign carried out by a larger, more experienced organization may take on a life of its own in the novice situation and overwhelm the whole campaign.

Not surprisingly, the threatening areas tend to be in the areas of personality, money, and structure. Leaders and advisers should be on the lookout for these:

Relying on do-it-all leaders. Many novice groups run on the energy of just one or two people, which is insufficient for a prolonged, deep campaign. Such a tightly led organization will have a difficult time expanding to meet campaign needs. Some members have been happy to allow others to carry the burden. Those carrying the burdens often prefer not to share control.

Seeking do-it-all leaders. Being victims of human nature, novice boards look for a few people to carry the campaign and then behave so ambiguously that the new people cannot get involved.

Interpersonal conflicts. Stress brings out the best in people and the worst. The same characteristics that have created and encouraged a powerful leader can become offensive when the campaign magnifying glass focuses in. Personality problems can abound, with the campaign becoming the ultimate victim.

Setting the goal too low. Full of fear, and thinking that "a little is better than nothing," the board may set a low goal that will make little impact on the future of the organization. Donor and volunteer commitment and enthusiasm are undermined by a do-nothing goal; campaign exhaustion cannot be justified by a great sense of success.

Asking too soon. Cultivation is a foreign concept to small organizations. The volunteers are so committed to the mission that they believe that the mission speaks for itself and that time spent cultivating donors is time spent away from fulfilling the mission. They also often find cultivation manipulative, because they do not realize the donor's need to learn more.

Soliciting from the bottom up. Novice organizations are not inclined to solicit major prospects first, and face-to-face. They are more comfortable with writing letters as a warm-up, which of course will not work to raise big gifts or change behaviors.

Insufficient skills. Most board members and staff members of small organizations have little experience in major-gift fundraising. These organizations require a great deal of hand-holding and training.

Letting the staff do it. Sometimes in their fear of changing, growing up, and gaining expertise, board members think they ought to let "the experts" conduct the campaign. In fact, although these organizations do need strong, perceptive professional counsel to create a link between passionate commitment and hands-on volunteer solicitation, their own sincere devotion is precisely what will motivate the donor.

Imagining easy ways to do it. All boards are hungry for an easy solution. The novices still hope to find one. The favorite shortcut temptations are these:

- Raise the funds through grants
- Divide the goal by the number of donors and get the same amount from everyone
- Send letters and just ask for more than last year

- Announce the campaign in the newspaper and wait for checks
- Run lots of communitywide special events
- Hire a fundraiser to do it

Ambivalence. Half the board thinks a campaign is too complicated, half that it is so simple they can do it without planning. Without strong guidance, these two will cancel each other out and gifts will never be asked for.

Energy problems. The novice group cannot withstand the normal ebbs and flows of a campaign and lets these patterns undermine their work and enthusiasm.

Designing campaigns for small organizations

Through careful strategic analysis of these characteristic problems, most organizations can develop a campaign plan that will assure success. Campaign planning in challenging situations requires tolerance and creativity. It calls for understanding organizational strengths—even when they are idiosyncratic—and finding ways to adapt proven campaign methods to the capabilities, potential, and strengths of the group.

Adapting proven methods takes time and patience, and it often frustrates the experienced professional. Yet a lack of tolerance of the underlying culture of an organization may deflate the passion and commitment that ultimately make a successful campaign possible.

Intelligent innovation that relies on thorough understanding of capital campaign fundraising, tempered by a knowledge of the realities of the organization, can enable development of a plan that utilizes passion and commitment to compensate for gaps in structure that would otherwise allow a more traditional campaign.

For the true grassroots organization philosophically opposed to tiered fundraising, an effective campaign plan will require at least a temporary change in the organizational culture. Generally, a compelling case for support is the most effective tool to stimulate real change in an organization's approach to fundraising. The process of developing a compelling case can bolster the energy of the volunteers and make the ends worth the risks. Once an organization feels deep ownership of the case, the board is likely to become pragmatic in pursuing those ends.

There are three approaches to adapting traditional campaign practices to the novice or nontraditional group: *bending tradition, tailoring solutions,* and *innovating.*

Bend tradition

In my survey of colleagues, my request for innovative techniques met with a staggering list of traditional methods that they have been able to bend and adapt to compatible behavior for the novices. The variations are mild, but definitely extensions of best practice principles.

Devise a plan. It is not enough to tell a grassroots organization that it needs a campaign plan. The group may never have created a plan before or worked within one, and the members may think they've done pretty well without one. These groups have to be coaxed into a detailed development of a campaign plan, eased through some unfamiliar territory, and given an opportunity to talk through challenges to the way things have been done before. Above all, my colleagues stress the need for involving key board and staff members in developing a strong, logical plan that provides adequate time for conducting the campaign effectively and efficiently. This usually requires a great deal of time devoted to prefeasibility and feasibility studies and to preparation. In some cases, the organization must repair years of haphazard or inadequate fundraising practices before tackling the campaign.

Do annual fundraising. Many small, young nonprofits would like to run a capital campaign even though they have no history of annual fundraising. Though not impossible, this is extraordinarily difficult. Many consultants encourage these organizations to provide adequate time to plan and conduct a modest annual campaign before undertaking the capital campaign, just to get the process started.

It is the rare capital campaign that gets organized faster than anticipated, and so the organization may even find it can get two annual drives completed before actually starting to solicit capital gifts. In just those two drives, many prospects will become donors, outreach will become cultivation, and the record system can be tested and assimilated.

Create leadership. In all campaigns, effective leadership is the sine qua non of success. Inexperienced groups know they need leadership but often don't know where to find it. The organization may have to grow its own leadership. This takes time. The shared responsibility for planning builds leadership that has been lacking. Therefore, it is most effective to bring the leadership candidates, particularly those who offer strengths not represented on the current board, into the discussion about the campaign very early. Through brainstorming and problem solving they will buy into the campaign more thoroughly.

Train. Though all staff and boards need training, boards of small inexperienced organizations need extensive training. On the positive side, however, these organizations are often more receptive to training than are more traditional, experienced, hierarchical boards. For one thing, they are fully aware of their inadequacies. Also, as a hands-on board that may have been overly involved in programming, a community or grassroots-type board may be more comfortable with role-playing and interactive exercises that work especially well for solicitation training. Their organizational culture may lend itself well to information-sharing, speaking their minds and hearts, and listening carefully to one another, which are all valuable characteristics in fundraising.

Offer more named giving opportunities. There is nothing unusual about named gifts in a capital campaign, but the naming is usually for buildings, endowments, and rooms. Lower-level donors can be encouraged to stretch high into the middle levels with named opportunities for smaller items: bricks in a path, trees in a garden, seats in an auditorium, for example.

Tailor solutions

There is a middle-ground between bending traditional campaign practices and creating new, innovative approaches. These require adapting traditional methods, tempered by an understanding of the organization and its strengths.

Foster nontraditional leadership. Whereas the perfect chairperson and key solicitors would be high-level donors themselves in a more traditional campaign, organizations with shallow donor pools will have to find their strength elsewhere. Deeply committed volunteers who simply don't have the wealth to provide leadership gifts may have the passion and devotion that will motivate donors at the highest levels.

Rely on phases. An organization may be staggered by the monetary goal but unwilling or unable to make the programmatic compromises necessary to lower the goal (such as, in a restoration project, doing without a ramp or elevator that is expensive but required for access). For such a group, conducting the campaign in phases over many years may be the solution. It is sometimes better to do this than to carry out several distinct smaller campaigns over those years, because the component parts of the project can be expressed in the case. Interim goals can be manageable and success gained, giving the organization credibility. Meanwhile, a willing and able major donor may be encouraged to make a more generous gift because of the overall size of the project. With phases, volunteers are less likely to burn out, and midcampaign slump is less likely to become midcampaign collapse.

Borrow power. It is the rare novice organization that counts real community power among its board members, but running the campaign without these leaders is a struggle at best. With a few well-placed introductions, exposure to the group's best successes, and a spirited personal plea, it is often possible to lure a highly visible, experienced fundraising volunteer to head up the campaign. This leader might never consider coming on the board or making another long-term investment but might rise to the challenge of helping to make a great first-time success.

When someone with deep community roots and powerful skills joins the effort, many others will come along as volunteers and donors. With luck, a few may stay after the campaign. But even if they don't, success is achieved. Ultimately, the organization grows from this "borrowed" strength and expertise.

Create champions. Employing lower-level givers as solicitors for major prospects is a nontraditional necessity for novice capital campaigners. If encouraged and trained, even a nervous solicitor who has demonstrated commitment with his or her own personal stretch gift and hard work can be very successful with a high-level prospect. The devoted volunteer who is able to bring in a major gift can become a model of success, inspiring colleagues to great heights. These champions often burst with enthusiasm and can help miracles happen in the campaign.

Invite miracles. Some miracles seem to occur in every capital campaign, but they are all the more obvious in first-time campaigns. Sometimes the adviser who "knows better" has to let the volunteers run with a wild idea, or even help develop their strategy. When there are little historical data, a volunteer's intuition may lead to remarkable success.

Innovate

In small organizations, invitations to invent occur repeatedly. Yet many advisers get stuck within a proven structure and cannot allow their boards the flexibility necessary to move toward these solutions.

It takes courage on the part of the adviser to endorse or suggest flexible methods. More than courage, it requires a deep knowledge of traditions before they can be put aside. But sometimes the unorthodox approach yields surprisingly successful and dramatic results.

Change the 80/20 rule. If the campaign study shows no prospects for the lead gifts on a standard gift range chart, the chart might be reconfigured to reflect a 60/40 rule. It is easier to complete a campaign with one disproportionately large gift, but that simply is not possible in many organizations. It may be more realistic to move a large group of midlevel donors up a few steps and create a plateau rather than a point at the top of the donor pyramid.

Do more face-to-face solicitation. There is usually a midlevel point on the gift range chart where face-to-face solicitation does not seem necessary, worthwhile, or possible. But because people tend to give larger gifts when asked to do so in person, training a larger solicitation corps and soliciting more prospects increases the number of larger gifts. In fact, in the novice organization there are likely "sleeper" prospects at the lower giving levels who simply have never been identified, cultivated, or asked for stretch gifts. Some don't even realize that the organization has great needs, because the asking has been so low-key and haphazard. Small organizations, with their abundant zeal, are often able to muster volunteers who, when trained, are willing and able to do a good job of soliciting a great many prospects in person.

Draft a highly visible staff member to cochair the campaign. Traditionally, volunteers make up the campaign committee. But in some cases, the distinctions between important volunteers and important staff blur; sometimes a longtime staff member or the director is so well-loved that he or she will be the most effective. Making that individual the campaign cochair helps everyone else on the campaign. Some reassignments of work are necessary when this position is recruited.

Make it a "public responsibility" campaign. Scary as it is to do so, announcing the campaign publicly before any funds are raised is a way to gain recognition for the case and the need. This bold move requires very careful planning and total readiness to plunge into major gift requests after the announcement is made, but it is also a way to encourage the community to take responsibility for the project. This is most effective in social service and other socially responsible causes, not cultural or educational projects; it relies on a sense of social urgency to meet the goal.

Start up the campaign with public funds. Some projects are candidates for public funds, including environmental, municipal, educational, and social service projects. From the onset it may be clear that public grants or bonds will make a project work. When an organization has no other prospects for lead gifts, it may be wise to combine public and private funds in the goal, obtain the public funds early, and announce the campaign after they are committed. In this way, an organization with little experience in capital campaigns can demonstrate early success and credibility.

Save individuals for the end. In addition to gaining federal and state grants, small or grassroots organizations might find it easier to raise money through a local bond, workplace pledges, corporate gifts, or foundation grants rather than through individual fundraising. These can jump-start the campaign.

A novice group is better off spending a year before the official campaign lining up these sources so the reliance on individuals is in keeping with the real potential. Even though a first campaign may raise a very small portion of its goal from individuals, the campaign process will be built for future annual and capital drives.

Let serendipity appear deliberate. Once in a while, a remarkable unexpected gift arrives on the doorstep: a bequest, a trust, a surprisingly large memorial gift. Campaign accounting policies for small organizations might be written broadly enough to give the board the option of rolling such a gift into the campaign. This may allow an increase in the goal and, in turn, result in raising donors' sights. These little surprises suggest similar stretches to donors and prospects, and they can offer the campaign a boost at just the right moment.

Focus on families. A young, inexperienced organization may find it impossible to attract a single gift large enough to top off its gift pyramid and inspire other donors. But it may be possible to obtain that gift if family members are approached together. People who are passionate about a cause are often willing to solicit other members of their families in order to raise a larger collective gift. They then set the pace for other families to join together and stretch toward a common interest, thus ratcheting up the organization's giving patterns higher than otherwise possible.

Collaborate with like-minded groups. Some novice fundraising groups have discovered that running a capital campaign in tandem with one or two other community groups is a highly successful strategy. Where there may have been insufficient visibility alone, the collaboration itself attracts attention. The shared goals and the impact of mutually advantageous programmatic or building efforts raises the community stake in the projects. Like using public funding, this is a way to establish a high enough goal so that donors think at major gift levels without putting the organizations at risk.

A shared campaign is also a means of linking organizations that could assist one another. For example, in one case, a senior center and a day-care center joined in building a multigenerational center. The wisdom and novelty of the project attracted a half-million-dollar gift from a known philanthropist who would hardly have noticed either campaign alone. That leadership gift provided the entire "quiet phase" of the campaign and gave the endorsement and credibility necessary to attract other new leadership prospects and gifts later.

Involve beneficiaries. Traditionally, the beneficiaries of a campaign are in the background, but they can be spectacular spokespeople for a campaign. For instance, in an affordable housing project for the elderly, an energetic eighty-five-year-old woman who hoped to live in the restored house spoke to a local service club along with the organization's director. No one in town forgot the heartfelt message she delivered. Similarly, for a youth center, teens can truly live up to high expectations when they become part of the fundraising team; furthermore, the benefits to them extend far beyond the value of the contributions.

Look the problems straight in the eye. We are all accustomed to campaign materials that feature beautiful plans for a future building. Another approach is to concentrate on current inadequacies and on illustrating the need. The board and the campaign committee should meet in the old site, but the prospects should see it too. A couple of hours viewing the current working conditions, the crowding, the inadequate facilities, and the dated equipment, will motivate many donors to stretch.

More at risk than money

There is no doubt that capital campaigns have a very significant impact on organizations. Even for the experienced group, a successful campaign makes incredible improvements possible whereas an unsuccessful campaign is a discouragement that affects the reputation for years. For first-time campaigners, the impact is far greater. It can change the nature of the organization itself.

It is not surprising that board members of small organizations are anxious as they begin their first campaign. Change is threatening, and a successful campaign may not mean just a new building: it may mean a new culture, new habits, new behaviors.

No organization can remain young forever. As it matures, an organization builds its institutional history, culture, and style. Individual founders and leaders play a role, but over time the institutional personality supplants them. A major campaign is a crucial moment in the organization's evolution; the real challenge is not whether to raise the money, build the building, or expand the fundraising, but whether the group can mature, professionalize, and still retain its spirit and passionate commitment.

The capital campaign itself can promise many advances for the organization that is anxious to grow:

For the staff. The campaign promises increased professionalism, more growth opportunities, livable salaries, educational opportunities.

For the board. It promises greater strength and awareness of governing responsibilities, more capacity to implement them, greater comfort and success with fundraising, and more likelihood of perpetuating the organization.

For funding. It will lead to more sophisticated and successful fundraising techniques with greater promise for annual, special, and capital campaigns in the future.

For public relations. A campaign can provide improved community visibility, wider acceptance of organizational goals, shared values, and good public image.

For the program. It promises more fully supported programs, and improved opportunities to achieve goals and accomplish the mission.

For the future. It promises a more sustainable future and the tools to secure it further, the potential for income from endowments, continued major gifts, planned gifts and bequests, and other support from a more aware and committed constituency.

In addition to all this, there is the intangible value of the community's validation of the organizational mission, style, and activities. The campaign can solidify the organization's position and importance in the community and root its value system within the local nonprofit sector.

Yet even though it gains these valuable improvements and stabilization, the wise nonprofit must hold tight to its original strengths. As it builds its technical, or "science" side, it must work harder to preserve the "art" of its existence: its spirit and commitment. The young organization has a relatively easy time describing its mission; as it matures, it should not let the mission be obscured. It is important not to grow up too fast and risk losing the clarity of vision, flexibility, and imagination that characterized the younger organization.

The wide-eyed naivete of youth is a terrific thing; though it allows for all kinds of trouble, it also invites great happy accidents, unimagined successes, and wild new ideas. These things are too good to lose, and may in fact be responsible for giving the board the courage to try a campaign at all. It would be a shame to allow a campaign and its learning experiences beat that innovative spirit out of a group.

A capital campaign is a high-risk opportunity for a fledgling organization. There is more at stake than raising money. A capital campaign has the potential to make or break a new organization. It must succeed in order for the newfound friends and donors to continue believing in the work of the organization. And it must succeed in order to reinforce the belief of the visionaries that this is work worth doing. Without that reinforcement, the spirit can be lost and bitterness can overtake the organization.

If the adviser has a solid background in traditional campaigning, he or she can help the organization value risk-taking, innovation, flexibility, naivete, energy, devotion, and obsession while learning new skills. The organization that plans its campaign around its own strengths, with full awareness of proven methodology and with informed courage and imagination to invent along the way, is the one that thrives. In fact, more than a few old, established institutions would do well to borrow a page from this book.

CHRISTINE P. GRAHAM *is a consultant to nonprofits in Vermont, where the nontraditional campaign is the most frequent choice. She is also the author of* Blueprint for a Capital Campaign *and* Keep the Money Coming.

Additional Resources

Brakeley, George A., Jr., *Tested Ways to Successful Fund Raising*. New York: Amacon, 1980.
An excellent overview written by one of the most successful consultants ever. Fifty years of experience, well distilled.

Dove, Kent E., *Conducting a Successful Capital Campaign*. San Francisco: Jossey-Bass Publishers, 1988.
Especially useful to large organizations; very well written. The principles described in 1988 remain true in 1998.

Fund-Raising Standards for Annual Giving and Campaign Reports: For Not-for-Profit Organizations Other than Colleges, Universities, and Schools. Washington, D.C.: Council for Advancement and Support of Education for the National Society of Fund-Raising Executives, 1998.
This long-awaited book will be an invaluable resource.

Kihlstedt, Andrea, and Schwartz, Catherine P., *Capital Campaigns, Strategies That Work*. Gaithersburg, Md.: Aspen Publishers, 1997.
An outstanding reference for community-based organizations. Well-organized information about every aspect of capital campaigning, written in a straightforward and engaging manner.

Quigg, H. Gerald, (ed.), *The Successful Capital Campaign, From Planning to Victory Celebration*. Washington, D.C.: Council for Advancement and Support of Education, 1986.
An excellent collection of articles, principally about higher education but applicable to others.

Rosso, H. A., and Associates, *Achieving Excellence in Fundraising.* San Francisco: Jossey-Bass, 1991.
The founder of The Fund Raising School describes his career with lessons for everyone who works in the fundraising field.

Seymour, Harold J., *Designs for Fund Raising.* (2nd ed.) Rockville, Md.: Fundraising Institute, 1988.
The first, and still classic, book on general fundraising principles and practices.

Index

opment process in, 26; geographical density of, 97; giving environment and, 39; in Vermont, 97–98. *See also* Small nonprofits
Not-for-profit organizations, 66. *See also* Nonprofit organizations

Objectives, of capital campaigns (example), 20–21
Off-the-shelf modules, 90
O'Neill, J. M., 35
Opportunity factor, 28
Organizational culture, 67
Organizations: development programs of, 67; goal setting and, 63, 66; higher goals of, 12; mature, 66; new, 66. *See also* Change, organizational; Effectiveness, organizational; Focus, organizational; Goals, organizational; Grassroots organizations; Mission, organizational; Nonprofit organizations; Not-for-profit organizations; Small nonprofits; Strategic planning, organizational; Voice, organizational

Pareto, V., 71
Passion, giving and, 39–40
Pennsylvania State University, The, 35
Perennially small organizations, 100. *See also* Small nonprofits
Personal information manager (PIM), 88
Philanthropy: campaign management systems and, 83; emotional basis of, 39, 83
Pierce, L., 5
Politics: board giving and, 16; planning participant selection and, 14
Press releases, 57. *See also* Publicity
Pressman, R. S., 91
Princeton University, 71–72
Prospect information systems: art-science combination of, 83–84; basic data in, 83–84; data gathering for, 84; donor categorization and, 85; donor staging and, 85–86; example of early, 82–83; gift range chart and, 82; in-depth data in, 84; moves management and, 85

Prospect management: definition of, 84; information management systems and, 90; pipeline concept of, 84–86; solicitation cycle and, 84–85. *See also* Development, donor
Publicity: development programs and, 69; donor recognition and, 56–57; on leadership giving, 56–57; press releases and, 57

Rosso, H. A., 23, 25, 30
Rule of Thirds, 71–72

Schreyer, B., 35
Schreyer, J., 35
Schwartz, C. P, 27
Seymour, H. J., 71, 72
Silverman, H., 35
Slogan, capital campaign, 20
Small nonprofits: categories of, 100–101; financial challenges of, 98; fundraising as art and, 99; grassroots organizations and, 100; perennially small organizations and, 100; start-up nonprofits and, 100–101
Small nonprofits, campaign design for: 80/20 rule and, 109; annual fundraising and, 106–107; approaches to, 106–112; bending tradition and, 106–108; beneficiaries and, 112; campaign phasing and, 108; champions and, 109; collaborative connections and, 111–112; compelling case and, 105–106; face-to-face solicitation, 110; family donations and, 111; flexibility/adaptation in, 105; fundraising plan and, 106; individual solicitation and, 111; innovation and, 109–112; key figures in, 110; leadership and, 107; meeting problems and, 112; miracles and, 109; named giving and, 107; nontraditional leadership and, 108; organizational culture and, 105; power and, 108–109; problem analysis and, 103–105; public funding and, 110–111; public responsibility issue and, 110; serendipity

"Unfolding the Promise," 72
University of Pennsylvania Law School, 35, 49, 54
University of Pittsburgh, 5
University of Richmond, 72
University of Southern Mississippi, 35
Urban Institute, 97

Van Dusen Endowment Challenge, 32
Vermont, nonprofits in, 98–99
Vision, organizational: CEOs and, 46; personalizing of, 19; strategic planning and, 19–20
Voice, organizational: identity statement and, 19; loss of, 11; reclaiming, 12
Volunteers: assignment of, 86; availability of good, 41–42; campaign

involvement of, 41–42, 54–55; concerns about, 41; development by organizations of, 42; development professionals and, 41; as donors, 43; impact of, 42; need for, 41

W. W. Kellogg Foundation, 31
Wang, C., 93
Ward, C. S., 5
Weill, J., 47
Weill, S., 47
Wertz, S., 35
Wharton School, 54

YMCA: capital campaign and Grand Rapids, 5; fundraising by NYC, 5

Back Issue/Subscription Order Form

Copy or detach and send to:
Jossey-Bass Inc., Publishers, 350 Sansome Street, San Francisco CA 94104-1342

Call or fax toll free!
Phone 888-378-2537 6AM-5PM PST; Fax 800-605-2665

Back issues: Please send me the following issues at $25 each
(Important: please include series initials and issue number, such as PF90)

1. PF _____

_____

_____

$ _____ Total for single issues

$ _____ Shipping charges (for single issues *only;* subscriptions are exempt from shipping charges): Up to $30, add $5^{50} • $30^{01}–$50, add $6^{50} $50^{01}–$75, add $7^{50} • $75^{01}–$100, add $9 • $100^{01}–$150, add $10 Over $150, call for shipping charge

Subscriptions   Please ❏ start   ❏ renew my subscription to *New Directions for Philanthropic Fundraising* for the year 19___ at the following rate:

     ❏ Individual $67   ❏ Institutional $115
NOTE: Subscriptions are quarterly, and are for the calendar year only. Subscriptions begin with the spring issue of the year indicated above. For shipping outside the U.S., please add $25.

$ _____ Total single issues and subscriptions (CA, IN, NJ, NY and DC residents, add sales tax for single issues. NY and DC residents must include shipping charges when calculating sales tax. NY and Canadian residents only, add sales tax for subscriptions)

❏ Payment enclosed (U.S. check or money order only)

❏ VISA, MC, AmEx, Discover Card #_____ Exp. date_____

Signature _____ Day phone _____

❏ Bill me (U.S. institutional orders only. Purchase order required)

Purchase order #_____

Name _____

Address _____

_____

Phone_____ E-mail _____

For more information about Jossey-Bass Publishers, visit our Web site at:
www.josseybass.com   **PRIORITY CODE = ND1**

Previous Issues Available